EVGENIDIS IOANNIS

The

HIDDEN TREASURES

of

BUSINESSES

DISCOVER the INCREDIBLE POTENTIAL of INTANGIBLE ASSETS

SERIES: KNOWLEDGE SHOTS

To my family with love!

ISBN: 979-8-70-681849-4

1st Edition February 2021

SYNOPSIS

What are the relationships that are being developed behind the numbers?

How brands, logos, copyrights, patents, IT applications, distribution channels, skills, relationships, human capital, communication, culture and many other 'intangible assets' affect corporate value?

What is the role of a business's customers, suppliers, shareholders and employees, in the discovery of its hidden treasures?

All this and much more, which ultimately contribute to corporate competitiveness and provide the fuel for the development of businesses, are described in a vivid and simple way....

This book is not a technical manual based on IFRS or other accounting standards. It aims to introduce the reader with simple concepts to the process of identifying the hidden treasures within businesses and the methods with which he can understand!!, highlight!! and measure them in order to maximize corporate value, turnover and profits!

Essentially this book is a 'value guide', a path way of exploiting all the intangible assets that exist within a business and that can lead to growth and prosperity.

So, let's discover them!

AUDIENCE FOR THE BOOK

The book you are holding in your hands can be useful to a multitude of readers.

It is not only aimed at specialized business executives. It is addressed to the whole world that deals with business from every possible angle!

Our goal from reading the book, is to benefit the following groups:

- Business owners of all shapes, entity and sizes,
- All employees in businesses regardless of their job,
- Executives, administrations and managers of organizations,
- Individuals interested in Selling, Buying and Merging Businesses,
- Economists, Accountants, Financial Analysts, investors of all kinds, from Venture Capitalists to Fund Managers as well as Specialists in Business Restructuring,
- Marketing and advertising department executives,
- Shareholders in companies, regardless of the percentage they hold,
- Students of schools of economics, marketing, business administration and any other professional field,
- Anyone who is interested in the more specific but also the general concept of 'business'.

CONTENTS

ABBREVIATIONS LIST

IC: Intellectual Capital

HC: Human Capital

SC: Structural Capital

RC: Relational Capital

IA: Intangible Assets

Q: Tobin's Q method

R&D: Research and Development

1. THE HIDDEN TREASURES OF BUSINESSES

Since ancient times even before the creation of the first economic relations, people have tended to store surplus goods so that they could use them later, when they considered it appropriate.

This has continued over the years. In most cases, they stored valuables so they would not be stolen and could be used in an emergency. The concept of the banking system did not exist at the time. People as entities were fighting for survival. Instinct was the primary element of life.

So gradually, the hidden treasures as we all have them in mind were created. Usually by pirates! Placed in chests, filled with gold coins, jewellery, pounds and many other valuables...

Humans have evolved since then. The structures of the economy have changed. We have now reached the knowledge-based economy, where we are being confronted with relentless global competition by globalization and stormy technological developments.

The heart of economic development is now businesses. As legal entities they are the link between human capital and economic development. Their aim is to develop the available resources. Their goal is prosperity! But does fuel to create a dynamic path exist? Yes, it does! But where will it be found?

Right next to us, within our reach. There are hidden treasures in every business! All we have to do is open the chest, point them out and make the most of them....

Knowledge, practices, habits, research, data, relationships, specializations, rights and more, which for owners, employees and other business executives are part of their daily work. But for others, these are all the missing pieces of the puzzle, the broken links of the chain on the way to development!

The assets of the businesses were traditionally of a material form. But now a new category is emerging very dynamically. That of intangible assets. These are the hidden treasures!

The ability of an organization to evolve in the market where it does business, to develop, to move forward dynamically, will ultimately depend on its ability to exploit these available intangible assets.

It is the intangible assets that will provide the business with a competitive advantage, add momentum to its action, ultimately increasing its valuation and its actual worth!

There are hidden treasures! They're still in the chest, waiting for us to dig them up, to sort them out, to distinguish and further analyze them, to bring them out again and finally to give value to our business!

Relationships behind numbers, employees, customers, suppliers, distribution channels, market shares, organizational culture, IT applications, procedures, technology utilization, any patents, trademarks, brands, logos, royalties, rights, favorable contracts, procedures, government licenses, partnerships, all that that leads to success and is taken for granted after being stifled by the routine of everyday life, ultimately contributes to corporate competitiveness and provides the fuel for development.

Intangible assets are becoming increasingly important in the modern business. They now determine its potential for value, for improvement, for enlargement, for growth.

In the end, intangible assets are the hidden treasures that lead us to competitive strengthening and give us corporate comparative advantages. So, let's discover them!

2. INTRODUCTION

In recent years, the values of 'Intangible Assets' have been increasingly discussed in businesses and beyond. They are the 'hidden treasures' that long to be exploited...

The economic changes that are happening around us are just a small part of a broader transformation, that of the transition from the production industry to today's knowledge-based economy, where businesses need to permeate into large consumer markets and where the development of competitive advantages has become the most important factor of success.

However, this requires an over-effort for continuous growth, high quality service provision, innovative solutions and customer focus. These needs are reinforced through free and at the same time global markets, leading businesses, particularly in recent years, to investing more and more resources in the capability to permeate, innovate and increase market shares.

As a result of these processes, most of the funds and resources available to organizations, are allocated to the preparation of 'modern' activities (for example in research and development, logos, trademarks, the "building up" of the brand through social media, employees training, distribution channels, supply chain, customer relations, technological – telecommunications infrastructure, etc.), rather than the well-known traditional business operation (such as the production, sales and simple delivery of finished products).

The investment of funds for the purpose of acquiring or developing intangible assets does not directly yield, does not create goods in the literal sense of the term. However, it lays the foundations for the creation of the final products or services which will serve the final consumer through the cooperation of these invisible elements.

At this point, some very interesting elements with regard to intangible assets need to be carefully assessed. First of all, it must be understood that the intangible assets must be combined with other elements of value. If a coherent combination of intangible and material factors is not achieved, the business will not be able to exploit the value expressed by intangible assets in its favor.

Another point that needs to be examined at a great scale is the fact that the value of intangible assets is linked to future business activity. This value represents the potential and ability of organizations to increase their activity, income and thus their profits in the future. The result is, the complexity of operating procedures in modern businesses, but at the same time they should manage to remain creative. More activities with potential for yield in the future, such as the development of new products and the continuous improvement of relations with customers, suppliers, etc. become an unbroken part of the operating model.

Everything around us is changing. The markets which businesses take activity in are constantly changing, but these aren't the only things changing. Together, the views of the owners and the corporate objectives that form the solid basis for the operating schemes are changing. To date, money and capital markets for intangible assets have not been created. More dynamic administration is now needed in companies, with eyes on the future...

This leads to the effort to create tools for 'quality' examination of the behavior of intangible assets, so that shareholders and company executives can understand their financial behavior, in depth.

In the modern economic status quo, the increased value of the importance of intangible assets is the decisive step. The characteristics of intangible assets are paving the way for business competitiveness, and if each business exploits them, it will optimize its activities and will achieve sustainable development.

Ultimately, the study of the practical and theoretical points related to intangible assets may contribute to the following objectives:

- Understanding the economic impact of such intangible investments on each business,
- The emergence of economic and qualitative data in the best interests of the company,
- Respect for innovation and technological change in order to create and maintain growth,
- The assessment of seemingly unconnected 'corporate knowledge, data and relationships', with market value.

3. DISTINCTIONS & CATEGORIES OF INTANGIBLE ASSETS

3.1 TANGIBLE AND INTANGIBLE ASSETS

In general, assets are goods that have a substance (material or intangible) and can offer economic benefits to a business. Fixed assets are broken down into two categories, tangible and intangible.

Fixed material assets «*are* *(fixed) tangible assets* *acquired by the business aiming to use them as means of action during its useful life, which is in any case more than one year*».

It's the assets that have material substance that we see, that we touch. Examples of such tangible fixed assets are buildings, plots, machinery, PCs, means of transport, furniture's, etc.

Intangible assets «*are those intangible economic goods which are subject to a monetary valuation and may be traded, either on their own or together with the economic unit*».

They are assets that have no physical substance, are invisible and abstract. Intangible assets are created or acquired with a view to their productive exploitation for a period of more than one year and are indicatively divided into the following categories:

1. Rights that can be used on their own (e.g., to be sold or rented and generate revenue, regardless of the operation of the business's entity), such as patents, logos, brand names, trademarks, copyrights, software and

2. Actual situations, properties and relationships, which usually cannot provide income on their own, but combined with each other or with other corporate functions, increase value and create comparative advantages, such as culture, training, reputation,

loyalty, good relations, proper organization of the economic unit, qualifications, specialization in the production of certain goods, presence in specialized markets and much more.

The second category includes the elements which make up, in particular, the meaning of the well-known term «capital gains» or «goodwill» of the economic unit which confer a total value greater than that resulting from the valuation of its individual assets.

According to another definition, an Intangible Asset is: «*Any fixed asset owned or controlled by a business, not in physical or financial form, but capable of providing future economic benefits*»[1]

In general, the main characteristics of intangible fixed assets are that they:

- have no physical existence and substance,
- guarantee their holder significant rights,
- provide the business with competitive advantages, and
- have a relatively long-life span.

3.2 CATEGORIZATIONS OF INTANGIBLE ASSETS

Many efforts have been made to properly categorize and through this, to provide a better description of intangible assets. As we have said, the term intangible broadly describes any economic element that has no material substance. Intangible elements are also referred to as invisible elements, or elements of knowledge.

A first form of categorization is as follows:

- **Marketing** (brands, trademarks, logos, trade names, domain names etc.),

- **Innovation** (patents, trade secrets, etc.),
- **Artistic** (copyrights, expression through books, music, poetry, theatre, etc.),
- **Technology** (software, information systems, proprietary technology, applications, etc.),
- **Operational** (Customer lists, niche markets, distribution channels, procedures, market shares, surveys, etc.),
- **Cooperative** (corporate culture, relationships with customers, suppliers, partners, etc.),
- **Finance** (royalties, leasing, etc.) and
- **Anthropocentric** (contracts with executives, training, leadership, relations between staff, etc.)
- **Privileged** (special government licenses, non-competitive contracts, government privileges, real options, etc.),

The above distinction covers most if not all of the intangible assets, but categorization efforts that can help simplify and understand them do not stop.

In the categorization we have just analyzed, it should be mentioned that the first four (4) categories relate to the so-called 'distinct' intangible assets. They are the ones that can be exploited on their own, generating income.

The last five (5) categories refer to intangible elements which for the most part cannot be exploited on their own, but only in combination and are usually expressed through the so-called 'goodwill'. They are 'indistinguishable' intangible assets or otherwise 'intangible phenomena'. And in these categories, we find assets that can be sold on their own (e.g., government licenses in some cases), but this is not the norm.

The concept of intellectual capital is also widely found, which is why another distinction between intangible assets may be the following:

- ✓ INTELLECTUAL Capital
- ✓ STRUCTURAL Capital
- ✓ RELATIONAL Capital
- ✓ HUMAN Capital.

3.3 CONCEPTUAL DEFINITION OF INTELLECTUAL CAPITAL

The conceptual link between Intangible Assets and Intellectual Capital was first recorded historically before 1850, when the economist *'Nassau William Senior'* referred to the 'IC' as a key factor of production.

However, the emergence of the 'knowledge-based economy' has been the core of the development of the field at a theoretical and practical level in recent decades. Knowledge is now transformed into a dominant prospect of value creation, with the 'IC' shaping the contexts of modern business reality!

One of the challenges every modern business is facing is the divergence between book value and market value. First '*Lev* (2001)' highlighted this systematic "gap" by showing that most of the market value is not reflected in the financial statements.

This observed "gap" between the corporate market and book value, demonstrates the inadequacy of the balance sheet. The 'IC' seems to be the driving force behind this divergence...

Definitions:

- «*Intellectual capital (IC) is the sum of hidden assets, which are not fully disclosed in the financial statements.*»[2]
- «*The IC refers to the invisible intangible assets that allow the operation of the business.*»[3]

- «*The IC includes all the critical factors for a business that are not presented in the balance sheet.*»[4]
- «*The IC includes corporate intangible assets which make up the vast majority of the market value.*»[5]
- «*The IC is often considered to be the difference between the accounting and market value of the company.*»[6]

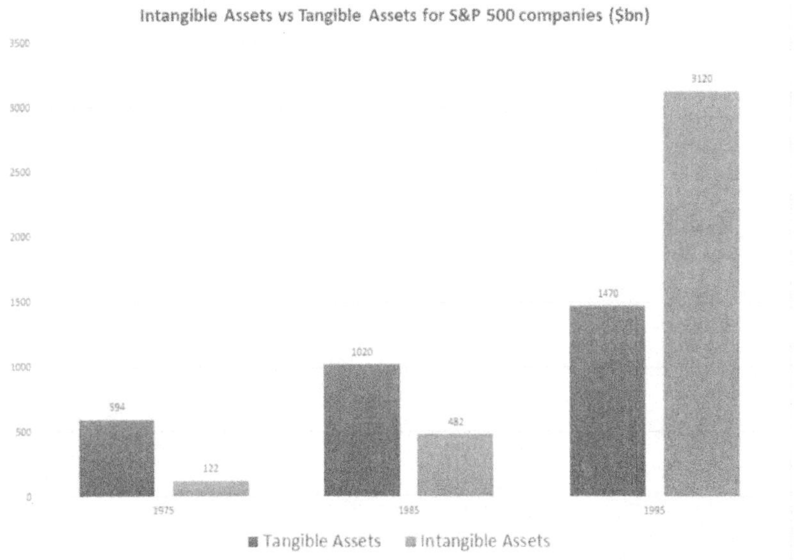

3.4 CATEGORIES OF INTELLECTUAL CAPITAL

The first fundamental category expressed by Intellectual Capital is that of "**Human Capital**" or "employee's competences" or "human-centered assets". This is an important factor as both the creation and dissemination of knowledge, which lead to competitive advantages, are fully dependent on this group of elements.

Human capital includes the knowledge, skills, communication, behaviors, relationships and creativity of employees. It is the mixture of knowledge, education, experience and business principles of individuals. "Human capital" is the heart of the IC, and reflects the knowledge of the company which, as we mentioned, is expressed through its human resources.

The second category of IC is that of "Structural capital" or "internal structure", which often appears to be identical or includes "organizational capital". At the same time, the closely related categories or subcategories of "innovation capital" and "technological capital" are of interest. This category is linked to anything that strengthens the human outcome. It is the glue and skeleton of organisms, since it provides the company with the means to maintain and disseminate knowledge. It encompasses all non-human reserves of coded knowledge, including an organization's corporate culture, strategies, structures, innovation, routines and processes. It's the intangible value that remains at the end of the day.

The third category concerns "**Relational capital**". It reflects the formation of relations with the environment. It reflects the potential for the business to evolve on the basis of its association with interested third parties: customers, suppliers, investors, institutions, banks, partners, entities, etc.

"**Spiritual capital**" is also very often expressed as "**Intellectual capital**". These concepts are linked, as the very significant advances in technology and telecommunications in recent years have structurally reorganized businesses, to make intangible assets a necessary condition for survival, creation and growth.

Intellectual capital is «*the spiritual material that has been formalized, captured and leveraged in order to create a higher value asset*» (Klein και Prusack, 1994). Intellectual Capital (IC) is also "*the knowledge that can be converted into profit.*»[7]

4. COMPETITIVE ADVANTAGES

4.1 COMPETITIVE ADVANTAGES & INTANGIBLE ASSETS

What exactly is a competitive advantage? What is its functional manifestation within a dynamic business?

When a business achieves returns (profit growth, turnover growth, cost reduction, etc.) that exceed the industry average and the averages of its main competitors, then we say it has gained a competitive advantage. Without it the business does not achieve its objectives and eventually declines.

Achieving a competitive advantage while being a business owner or executive is an easy step. The hard part is to get your competitive advantage to be sustainable for a long time.

In fact, it is even more difficult to achieve a set of comparative advantages, which will work as feedback for each other and will result in even greater corporate returns.

Through intangible assets, the comparative advantages of businesses are greatly magnified, offering the differentiation which is necessary in today's knowledge-based economy and specialization.

Intangible assets are the critical qualitative factors that create value, competitive advantages and develop businesses regardless of their size. They are their hidden treasures!

4.2 CONCEPTUAL APPROACH TO COMPETITIVE ADVANTAGE

Without achieving a competitive advantage, the business has no reason to exist! It will truly neither prosper nor grow. The

competitive advantage is the quality characteristic that will eventually lead to an increase in both the turnover and profits of a business. It's the gateway to prosperity. It is the element that gives the impetus for the economic growth that each organization is looking for.

But how is a competitive advantage actually gained? Very often through technological developments. The use of some technological innovations gives us a head start over competition. Usually, however, competition manages to implement the same innovation or an even more innovating approach in a short period of time. So technological innovation is useful, it helps evolution, it takes us to the next step, but it doesn't keep a business up for a long time.

Competitive advantage becomes sustainable when based on different characteristics compared to technological innovation. What are these? Emotions! All these symbols, concepts and images that a product 'engraves' on the final consumer, constitute the great and sustainable competitive advantage.

The experience of a customer acquiring a product is irreplaceable and cannot be easily copied. The importance of goods for society is also a very important feature. More and more corporate strategies are trying to give customers the conceptual importance of a product and not so much its characteristics. They are trying to give the so-called 'personal importance' to its use. Emotions are therefore the modern method of selecting products and connecting with the customer.

Another point that can give us a competitive advantage is the cost. If there is the possibility of producing a product of the same quality but of lower cost in relation to the competition, it certainly gives us a significant advantage.

If, on the other hand, a business offers products of greater value than the competition but of different improved characteristics, then it applies the 'diversification' technique. Through the process of

diversification, an exceptional corporate competitive advantage is created and at the same time, value is added to the business and its customers.

4.3 APPLICATION OF THE COMPETITIVE ADVANTAGE

A business must not rest on a comparative advantage. It must constantly strive for the development of new ones, but also for the enhancement of existing ones with the aim of maximizing their lifespan.

An organization should never stop its evolution in one field. It must develop the forms of a competitive advantage in other new activities.

Comparative advantages are directly linked to intangible assets and intangible economic phenomena. In trying to give them a specific form we can mention the following:

- *Brand and trade names.* Strong brand = long-term competitive advantage. In fact, it has been observed that strong brand name leads to greater value in products and thus to higher profits.
- *Patents.* An important source of competitive advantage. Any innovation, especially if it can be copyrighted, leads the company to becoming a leader in its area of expertise.
- *Distribution network.* Properly organized distribution network = excellent customer service.

- *Market share*. The greater the market share, the smaller the space for competition to develop.

All this is just the tip of the iceberg. Competitive advantages are closely linked to intangible assets. One fuels the other and together they take corporate growth to the next level.

5. DISCUSSING FOR INTANGIBLE ASSETS

5.1 UNDERSTANDING INTANGIBLE ASSETS

How can a business comprehend its intangible assets? How can it distinguish them in the uproar of daily work and through everyday effort?

There are some questions, that by being answered, an organization understands the intellectual capital it holds. These are the following:

1. *What competitive advantages does the company have?*
2. *Have they been recorded? How are they reflected in everyday corporate work?*
3. *Who owns the rights of use – exploitation?*
4. *How could the company take advantage of them more fully?*
5. *To what extent is the performance-risk ratio defined?*

Just as administrations and corporate executives are aware of tangible fixed assets (buildings, machinery, equipment), they must also recognize the characteristics of intangible assets. This is because if administration and employees fail to recognize, among other things, the value, dynamics and supply of all its assets, any development planning cannot be successful.

The assessment of the value of intangible goods can be quantified more easily for discrete intangibles, i.e., trademarks, patents, software and intellectual property.

But not all situations are the same. Intangible assets such as developing partnerships and 'Know – How', potential talents, knowledge and skills of the workforce, training procedures, special technical knowledge, expansion into specialized markets, etc., while of great importance, they are considerably difficult to value and thus to state precisely how much they contribute to the turnover and results of the business.

In conclusion, failure to provide specific and clear answers to the above questions also entails an unsuccessful assessment of intangible assets.

5.2 THE IMPORTANCE OF INTANGIBLE ASSETS

When we talk about intangible assets, we must keep in mind that they cannot be easily identified, their 'nature' is elusive. The brand name, logos, customer lists, IT applications and ultimately knowledge, intellectual capital in a sense, confer significant economic value despite the fact that little is recorded in accounting and therefore there can be no official and accurate information.

However, the importance of intangible assets is enormous for any business (large, medium, small or even very small). Intangible assets are those that lead to evolution and thus to competitive advantages. They are the hidden treasures that all business units seek.

That is why intangible goods are now dynamically introduced into the designs of innovative businesses. After the investment of funds in the material fixed assets, plots, buildings, machinery, PCs, furnitures and generally the necessary infrastructure equipment, intangible assets come to transform them into development. If these are absent, the fixed assets on which a company has invested cannot be exploited and return turnover and profits.

Globalization brings about changes in all kinds of economic life. Trade is constantly changing, consumer habits are changing. There are no barriers between countries anymore. Transport is also evolving rapidly. All this creates a suitable ground for continued growth in transactions and communication around the world.

The production of business products is often done in combination in many countries. Multinational companies have factories everywhere. Parts of the goods that are produced in one country are being assembled in another and are being sold on a different market.

In this model of operation and growth, the huge development of technology, and the reduction in the cost of telecommunications, has contributed. This creates goodwill chains in many sectors of the economy.

Therefore, corporate culture, knowledge developed, distribution channels, niche markets, brand names and more, are sources of competitiveness. Businesses are forced to take part in a race. They invest in the permeation of specific – new markets, the improvement of employees, the design of brands, distribution channels, and market shares and finally the improvement of products and new technological applications. For these reasons, the importance of intangible assets is constantly growing within businesses.

5.3 INTANGIBLE GOODS AS VALUE GUIDES

In today's economy of knowledge and information, the real values of a business are not fully expressed in its financial data. Ownership of some important intangible assets such as good relations with partners (clients - suppliers), communication of employees, presence in specialized markets, training of staff, etc. cannot under any circumstances be taken for granted.

However, although they do not belong exclusively to the business, combined with each other or on their own, they develop a great value which cannot be seen at first glance. Despite the efforts of economists and other scientists, there is no easy way to accurately assess all this data emerging through a dynamic business.

If the business model is successful, if the company generates turnover and profits, it should not necessarily be interested in the monetary value of intangible assets. Intangible assets are mainly 'quality value indicators' and as such we must analyze them with a view to both the present and the future.

While it may be illusory, perhaps even tricky, for businesses to develop values in intangible goods without the existence of markets that could confirm – value them accurately (e.g., specific stock exchanges for intangible assets), there are some non-economic – qualitative indicators which could shed a great deal of light on the characteristics of intangible assets and become 'value guides'.

Historically, companies have used information systems (MIS), which were based solely on economic data. In recent years, advanced information systems have allowed for a more comprehensive picture of the evaluation of a business. Even now, however, they deliver a report mainly on economic data, while quality indicators remain idle.

Growth of Intangible Assets and Tangible Assets for S&P 500 companies ($bn)

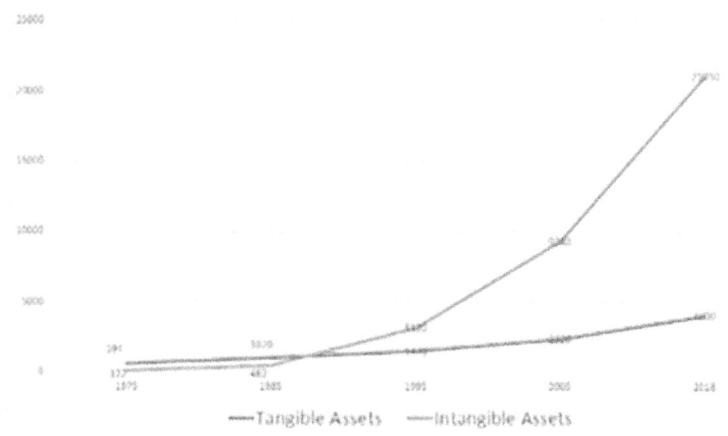

It must become the primary objective of business executives to record and develop constituent elements and business drivers of their value. In the past, organizations used natural resources,

buildings, equipment, etc. The term 'intellectual capital' has now entered the corporate culture as the advanced guide to analyzing the relationships between growth resources and value creation in a business.

The companies never act by themselves as a 'value guide', but in essence it is the services and resources they offer as well as their human capital.

5.4 HIDDEN VALUES IN MODERN BUSINESS

Many businesses recognize their life circle, when it has already happened. But they become successful not when they close their old life cycle, but when they open the new one!

At this time of change, it is necessary to decide on the corporate transformation and the change of structures. The aim should be to create a new modern flexible partnership, which will enhance their position in the market as well as the size of the business, while at the same time freeing up over-value, generating synergies and maximizing returns.

Accelerating these operational developments, growth prospects are enhanced and hidden corporate values are being brought to the fore, the hidden treasures of businesses that have not been evident to employees and shareholders until now.

These changes create benefits and values at the cost level, enhance economies of scale, optimize procurement, homogenize the management of human capital and bring operational synergies.

These new schemes must have the critical size, deep knowledge and experience, strategic superiority, economic and bargaining power to be able to respond to the dynamics and continuous rotations of international markets.

It is therefore found that there is a hidden value that is not easy to understand, it could be characterized as intangible, but it is completely true!

The values of businesses, even the world's largest ones, are now significantly higher than the value shown on their balance sheets. It is obvious that the elements that give companies the value they possess are not their facilities, furniture's and mechanical equipment, but the know-how, the skills of its employees, the potential of the leadership, technological innovations, etc.

It follows, therefore, that the real value lies mainly in elements of intangible form, especially in knowledge and in human resources.

Employees may not have to work daily with a physical presence in their workplace, but to work with colleagues, customers and suppliers through computers and networks. In fact, this organizational culture is constantly gaining ground.

Brands, copyrights, patents, etc., highlight the identity of the company and represent greater value than its equipment and facilities. Business is conducted in a digital environment (Internet) where customers are served through technology. So, if we were to eliminate from the concept of business computers, emails and knowledge of how to use technology, it probably would not function productively.

If the knowledge of the employees is lost, it will take years to replace. If the brand is lost, the company will lose value. It is obvious from all these that for most companies the hidden value is not in the material assets but mainly in the intangible!

Intangible assets usually have little value when they are individual (with the exception of 'discrete intangibles' such as patents, brands, copyrights, software and perhaps 1-2 more). However, they create significant added value, when they affect each other in a context of other quantitative or qualitative factors!

The value is ultimately not created by each intangible element individually, but by the successful combination of many together, making the process multiplicative as opposed to additive!

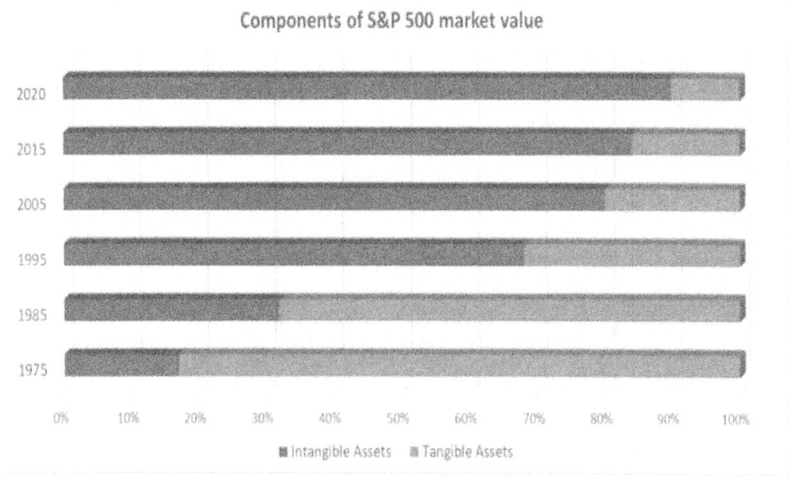

5.5 INTANGIBLE ASSETS AND FINANCIAL RECOGNITION

Competitive advantages do not evolve into a business with ease. It takes a lot of effort to get them, to develop them, to bring them out and finally to take advantage of them. Comparative advantages can be offered by both material and intangible assets.

Material fixed assets mainly need capital. Intangible assets, however, have some unique properties. They link material assets to corporate development!

Compared to material resources that are accounted for, intangible resources are much more likely to be the catalysts for achieving corporate competitive advantages. The productivity of a company is located to a greater extent in its intangible assets than in its physical equipment.

So, it is perfectly reasonable to assume that profitability and growth are directly related to the exploitation of Intangible Assets in a company.

Balance sheets offer useful information not only to banks and analysts but also to any interested parties. However, this information should also be able to be used by future investors. Therefore, events and incidents which may affect not only the current but also the future economic course of an organization should be reported in its balance sheet.

Financial accounting case law, however, throughout the world has established rules for the measurement and presentation of materials in relation to intangible fixed assets. The big question that arises, for example, is when and how, the development costs of intangible assets should be recognized as expenses in the financial statements.

There are two 'points' which seem to be the main elements which affect the recognition of intangible assets in the accounting statements and we must highlight them.

1. The '*timing*': The costs of developing an intangible asset can be incurred long before the potential future benefits are proven and highlighted. The subject of discussion of economic scientists is, in which accounts these costs should be registered.
2. The 'contact point': The link between the development costs of intangible assets and the benefits that the company will ultimately have, cannot be genuinely and directly

3. established. On the contrary, for fixed assets this can be more easily demonstrated.

Of all the intangible assets, brands, copyrights, patents and IT applications have been significantly researched. However, 'non-discrete' intangible assets have been less researched.

In the case of 'non-discrete' intangible elements there is a large lack of official data. Here a gap is discovered that needs solutions and must be filled adequately.

5.6 DIFFICULTIES IN ASSESSING INTANGIBLE ASSETS

Intangible assets are very important and should appear on the balance sheets of economic units. In this way, a financial and substantial picture of the company would be brought out.

However, the evaluation of intangible assets presents various problems in relation to tangible fixed assets (buildings, machinery, etc.). The next are considered to be of utmost importance:

A*)* *Construction*. Intangible assets are difficult to «capture». While the material fixed asset has a specific and measurable form, concepts such as partnerships, education, competitiveness, customer relations, employee satisfaction, etc. are difficult or even impossible to quantify.

B) *Emergence*. Due to the need to make significant investments in order for intangible assets to start to emerge and to return value, important questions arise. At what point does this investment pay off and the intangible good creates value? In fact, when is it maximized?

C) *Inability to separate benefits*. There can be no separation and exclusion from the benefits generated by intangible assets. Their advantages can also be extended to entities that have not invested in them. For example, an employee who trained in one business, after a long time he will be working for another. The benefits of his skills are reaped by the second business without it having invested in him as much as the first one.

5.7 COMMON WAYS OF EXPLOITING INTANGIBLE ASSETS

But how can we achieve the exploitation of an intangible asset or a group of them in order to improve cash flows?

There are several methods by which we, as owners, executives and employees of a company, are able to exploit our intangible assets.

We present, for example, the following cases:

1. Possibility of selling the intangible asset.
2. Royalties from providing the use of intangible goods to third parties (e.g., licensing for the use of a company's brand, granting of patents for a specific time, etc.).
3. Merge or strategic alliance with other businesses, with the common objective of developing economies of scale and exploiting greater opportunities for action.

The examples above are by no means the only ones. But they are the most common, as they show typical cases where the exploitation of intangible assets takes place, increasing both the chances of success and of course the risk of failure for the business.

We must never forget that intangible assets, intangible economic phenomena and the competitive advantages created through them, are the hidden treasures of our business. It is up to us to highlight and complete theire exploitation!

OPENING THE CHEST

OF

THE HIDDEN TREASURES!

6. MARKETING INTANGIBLE ASSETS

6.1 INTRODUCTION TO BRANDS & TRADEMARKS

Brand names, logo, trademarks, etc. are the most important intangible assets of large companies. And nowadays, even for small businesses they are an important asset and receive special attention.

Brands, firms, logos and trademarks, along with copyrights, software, applications and patents, are distinct intangible assets and in recent years the legal registration process has been extensively developed.

Historically, brands have been introduced first. Evidence suggests they appeared about 5,000 years ago, originally in ceramics! The first attempts at legal registrations appeared in Roman law, but mainly with the aim of protecting customers from illegal products.

Brands are not just names written on a piece of paper or words illuminated on a label. They are the feelings expressed by a product, the very culture of the organization. That's why businesses are rushing to secure them, as it is now becoming important for their present and future. If they are left free for use and are not protected, they offer competitors copying capabilities, thus making organizations lose part of their uniqueness.

A big role in the development of ideas behind brands and logos is played by the development of marketing, the power of television, the evolution of advertising, the speed of messages via the Internet, social media, changes in international rules, standards and globalization. Everyone nowadays is taking care of the brand name...

In recent years there has even been a new industry that is developing, that of measuring the performance of brands. It is the evolution of the use of trademarks and the importance it has acquired. Brand names, logos, symbols, titles and trademarks are now one of the largest and most important intangible assets for any business. It's a hidden treasure! Any attempt to achieve a competitive advantage is strictly linked with their protection, promotion and development.

6.2 BRAND DEFINITIONS

Brand name «*is a name, term, symbol or design, trade mark, logo or combination thereof, designed to identify the products and services of a business and to differentiate them from those of competitors.*»[8]

A brand name usually consists of a name and in many cases is combined with a design, a shape and other characteristics (e.g., a particularly unique packaging).

Brand names are part of the so-called added value, 'goodwill' of a business and belong to the distinct intangible assets that can be exploited (purchase, sale, rental, etc.) even separately in some cases.

The brand name always contains uniqueness. That makes the business stand out. Through it, it differentiates itself from the competition and the identity of the goods it produces. Sales of well-known brands are now observed to be much higher than others with lesser-known brand names (e.g., anonymous labels).

For all these reasons it is necessary to legally register the labels of businesses in each market, whether we are talking about products or services. In addition, we succeed in this way in cutting off competition from possible use of these in the future by making it illegal.

Brands essentially affect consumers. They manage to become part of themselves. The choice of products of a brand is related to how each consumer recognizes himself. This relationship should not be

overlooked in any case. Psychological factors play a big role in product choices now. Everyone's personality is linked to brands and those brands to us...

The specific relationship that develops is the set of ideas, and values that the good offers. It is not only the characteristic elements. It is not just the benefits it offers. More information is needed for the customer to choose. Emotions!

6.3 BRAND IDENTITY

The basic characteristic of a brand is its uniqueness. This uniqueness determines the so-called 'identity' in the brand name.

The brand, the logo, the tradename, don't come from nothing. They have a past that should not be underestimated. This past, the changes in which it has been fermented, the important moments that have affected it, all the aura around its evolution, are its legacy. In fact, many times this heritage is universal and sometimes it is local. But it doesn't matter. Its power remains unchanged.

Trademarks express specific purposes and values. They are a set of expectations on the part of consumers. Marketing greatly influences the development of this consciousness. Candidates and loyal customers want to feel confident. They want 'confirmation' of the benefits that will result from the use of the products and services. This is the role of advertising, i.e., communication between the company and the consumer, to bridge this gap. To prove by convincing customers of the benefits that will result and asking for proof of their benefits.

The ad intends to communicate positive effects. These are not only designed for TV, radio, social media or the internet. Even on the packaging of the products designs, colors, shapes etc. are included, which have the same goal. To certify the authenticity of the benefits.

A brand, regardless of the extent to which it is known and highlighted, has identity and character. This identity, this special character is what sets it apart from the competitors. A brand has distinctiveness and offers unique benefits.

The 'identity' of the brand is a hidden treasure for businesses. But it's not enough just to discover it. We must also use it for the benefit of our business!

6.4 RECOGNITION OF THE VALUE OF BRANDS

A brand can be exploited in order to offer cash flows, usually through sale or acquisition. This is not just about operative businesses. It also concerns companies that remain inactive or in a cease-and-down regime for many years and which have a significant 'brand name' or even logos that are sought after.

Since it can generate income, a brand is a distinct intangible asset. Therefore, it should be valued by scientific methods and displayed in the official economic data. Yes, a name, a title, a trade mark, a symbol, is an asset for a business of every size and should not be neglected.

For these reasons, entrepreneurs and executives, mainly of large and medium-sized businesses, claim to present the value of the brands in their published financial data, with a view to:

• *Improving the value of the capital and the financial balance sheet data in general.*

• *Improving the equity ratio in relation to borrowed funds and*
• *Positively affecting the price of shares in the event of listing in the stock market.*

On the other hand, it is practically difficult to assess brands separately from the businesses. It takes special knowledge and experience for the assessor to achieve this and to be able to prove it on the basis of objective criteria.

The value of a newly purchased brand, as well as the goodwill that accompanies such moves, affect the results of the balance sheets. Acquisitions and mergers are a tool of efficiency for the markets and as such, are given special attention by economic scientists.

6.5 THE GOODWILL OF THE BRAND

The brand offers goodwill to businesses. The customer perceives it, feels it and experiences it in terms of benefits and emotions. It has an effect not only on him, but undoubtedly on his choices.

Consumers are now demanding. But they can also be affected. They evaluate not only the usefulness of the goods, but also the ideas behind them.

The main objective of the brands is to achieve the so-called 'loyalty' of customers, i.e., to remain faithful to the products that emerge behind the ideologies of the brands. High brand value means loyal consumers to the ideals the brand stands for.

Businesses want the consumer to remain loyal to them. If this is the case, the goodwill of the brand is demonstrated.

They emphatically ask to emotionally connect with the customer in order to maximize their loyalty. They're fighting to make their brand a slogan. Thus, they achieve not only increased turnover but also a decrease in the sales of their competitors.

Brands offer corporate goodwill. It is up to the owners, shareholders, executives and employees themselves to be able to maximize their value. Brands are a hidden treasure. The spotlight tools are there. Let's make the most of them!

7. INNOVATION INTANGIBLE ASSETS

7.1 DEFINITION OF PATENT

In today's knowledge-based economy, information is overabundant. It takes a lot of effort to discover the 'substance' behind this stream of data overwhelming us.

Creativity cannot be excluded, it cannot be trapped. In combination with 'information' and in addition to knowledge and experience, it ultimately leads to innovation.

Inventions, modernisms and innovations essentially take humanity to higher levels. But they also offer income to those who make it. In order to make the most of it, it is of course necessary to legally protect them. This is achieved through patents.

To the inventor, the legislator therefore offers as a possibility the 'patent'. It is the exclusive right to use the patent for the specific discovery and may concern either a natural or a legal person.

This exclusive option is usually granted for 3 to 20 years (depending on the place and time) from the application for legal protection and prohibits others from using this discovery without the permission of the inventor. This definition is an important expression for the protection of rights.

Patents protect the ownership of the creator's idea or innovation in its development process and thus facilitate the realization of the product.

It is understood from the above that the basic condition for the provision of protection in a patent, is that it should concern a creation of the spirit belonging to the broader concept of invention.

The holder of the diploma may be one of the following:

1) *The real inventor.* The right to obtain a patent is granted to the person who created the invention or the holder of the patent.
2) *One or more inventors.* If the invention was invented by more people and there was no initial agreement between them, the right belongs to everyone indivisibly. If the invention was carried out by more people who worked separately, priority is given to the first person who made the application to acquire the right of use, or to the one who takes precedence over others or even collectively under pre-conditions.
3) *Inventions made by employees.* In the case of an employee's patent in a business, a percentage of this belongs to the company and another percentage to the employee (usually 40%-60% but it depends each time).

7.2 REASONS FOR PATENTING

Patents have very important purposes and objectives.

The first purpose is to **motivate**. A human by nature seeks motivation reward. With the innovation, research and discoveries that they entail, it benefits not only the inventor but also society more broadly as a whole.

The second purpose is to **publicize innovations**. Why not keep patents secret so that competition doesn't know them? This issue is resolved by the right of patent. By delimiting this right, the possibility of the inventor behaving monopolistically is downscaled.

In order to obtain a patent, the inventor must disclose the invention in detail giving analytical information. In this way, the benefit is exchanged between him and society.

The inventor acquires rights of use and thus profits for many years and society benefits from the creation of the development of new ideas.

Innovation and patent protection are a powerful tool for expanding the *competitive advantage of every business.*

7.3 LAW FRAMEWORK OF PATENT

What does the patent ultimately offer to someone who patents it? It offers him the following:

α) to produce and exploit the discoveries himself and
β) to prohibit others from using his inventions, unless he expressly so allows,

In the event that there is an infringement by a third party of the patent right, the law provides the holder with certain important capabilities:

α) *Claim to remove the contestation*. This claim destroys or withdraws from trade, products which affect the right of the beneficiary.
β) *Claim for damages*. The holder may claim sums of money in the event of infringement of the patent right.

γ) *Declaratory lawsuit*. With the declaratory lawsuit, the person who has the exclusive license to exploit the patent may also bring the above claims, as well as the person who has applied for a patent and expects to obtain the right.

7.4 ADVANTAGES & DISADVANTAGES OF PATENTS

The main **advantage** of the patent system is the offer of incentives for innovation, research and development.

Also, the advantages for the patent holder are that it minimizes the risk. In short, it gains an advantage over competition for this reason.

It still protects him from any attempt at falsification because he is now legally covered.

Finally, it gives the inventor social prestige and, of course, the opportunity to have economic benefits, either by taking advantage of the invention himself, by selling it, or even by renting it!

As far as **disadvantages** are concerned, they are small but we must not neglect them.

Usually inventions, until they are exploited and generate positive cash flow, have a high cost. It is therefore necessary in many cases to initially make available a significant amount of capital with a doubtful final result.

Moreover, in cases where the competition tries to falsify or copy a patent, litigation has significant costs and is a waste of time. So here too it is necessary to be able to provide liquidity for the inventor.

Finally, one phenomenon that is increasingly appearing is that businesses are fighting for new discoveries, and could well work together by developing mutual benefits and synergies for all.

7.5 TRADE SECRETS

Trade secrets are confidential data of any kind (production, technical texture, financial, organizational secrets, etc.), which allow their holder to increase his income, avoid unjustified costs, to gain market leadership or to obtain commercial benefits, but without having legally protected them.

Examples of trade secrets: financial informations, used procedures, secret formulas, techniques or technical know-how, customer base, innovations and general information for which the owner prefers not to disclose.

Usually, a trade secret becomes the subject of a confidential agreement. The main reason why some companies do not want a trade secret to be revealed, is because they do not want to have time commitment and limits, to exploit their discovery.

Trade secrets cannot be ideas, designs and informations if they are not completed in any material form (documents, samples, etc.). Nor can any information be treated as a trade secret, if its owner is not a legal entity.

8. ARTISTIC INTANGIBLE ASSETS

8.1 BASIC CONCEPT OF COPYRIGHTS

Intellectual property is the rights acquired by its owner on the work that he created and legally protected.

Creator

«The creator of a spiritual work is considered to be the one whose name is on the work.»[9]

Even if the creator is referred to through a nickname, as long as the connection of that nickname to the person is known, it is recognized under these conditions.

Work

«Work means any original intellectual creation of speech, art or science, expressed in any form, in particular written or oral texts, musical compositions with or without text, plays with or without music, choreography, architectural works, audiovisual works, photographs, works of visual arts including drawings, paintings and sculptures, engravings and lithographs, works of applied arts, illustrations, maps and all three-dimensional works relating to geography, topography, architecture or science.»[10]

Also works are any collections, adaptations of works, other alterations thereof, as well as encyclopedias, anthologies and databases, but only if they are original.

There are enough limits to the exploitation of a work by its creator. Within the EU, copyright protects the creator up to 70 years after his death. Outside the EU, in those countries that have signed the Berne Convention the minimum time limit is 50 years from the author's death, while the maximum varies.

Copyright is an important intangible asset and should be given special attention. Sometimes it is considered a given, but it is a treasure for every business that owns it and must be used in any case. Its importance is enormous.

8.2 HISTORICAL REVIEW OF COPYRIGHTS PROTECTION

The protection of Intellectual Property has existed as a concept for a long time, as strange as it may seem to us.

First of all, from antiquity to the middle Ages there is no indication of its presence, due to the fact that there was not yet the technical possibility to obtain copies of spiritual works.

It all started in Ancient Greece. There was initially the creator connected through his name with his work. When something illegal happened in connection with this incident, the exploiter was charged and sanctioned, legally and ethically. In fact, there was a presentation of artistic works in special competitions! There, a prize was offered to each successful candidate.

Rules for the protection of intellectual property initially emerged due to the need created by technological development. Since it has become easy by technical means to produce copies, there has been a need to institutionalize copyright. The development of technology was the catalyst for intellectual property.

A first arrangement occurred after the invention of typography by Gutenberg (1448 A.D.). The first privileges were given to printers in Venice in 1469 and later to other European states (from 1500 A.D. onwards).

The aim at the time was to protect the capital investment of the printer and not the creator of the work. This was achieved later, with the spring brought about by the French revolution in all ideas and freedom of expression.

The great legal leap was finally made to the law passed in France in 1791 (Le Shapelier Law), which established the first copyrights for the author of the work. At that time the rights lasted even five (5) years after his death.

8.3 INTERNATIONAL CONVENTIONS FOR THE PROTECTION OF COPYRIGHTS

International Convention Berne - Paris

The Berne-Paris International Convention is the most important international treaty for the protection of intellectual rights. It was signed in 1886 in Berne, Switzerland, and with it the foundations were laid at international level for the protection of intellectual property.

The basic principle of the Berne Convention is that of the assimilation of foreign authors with the inhabitants of the country where protection is sought. The last revision of the Convention was in 1971.

Rome International Convention

The Rome International Convention was signed in 1961 in the city of the same name. It became known because it was the main international treaty for the protection of related rights.

The Treaty essentially recognized the three categories of beneficiaries of related rights: executants (otherwise performers), producers of phonograms and broadcasters.

TRIPS Agreement

The moment when intellectual property, the globalization of markets and technological change met, the big bang happened! TRIPS Agreement tried to give the solution.

This agreement concerns intellectual property rights in the field of trade. This Agreement is included in the Final Act of the Uruguay Round (1994).

The TRIPS Agreement has been binding in most countries since 1996 and has a scope that now covers both industrial and intellectual property.

WIPO Treaties

WIPO Treaties are also known as Internet Conditions. They concern, inter alia, intellectual property and interpretations – executions of phonograms. Improve the existing arrangements of the International Conventions of Bern and Rome and by going beyond the TRIPS Agreement, they provide solutions to some of the problems created by digital technology.

Wipo Treaties give creators wider intellectual property rights than those of the Berne International Convention, but at the same time try to solve problems created by new technologies.

In particular, what is expressly recognized and established is the right to lease copyright, the protection of computer programs and databases, the right to distribute. They try to cover the on-demand transmission of works, obligations are imposed with regard to technical protection systems and the provision of information on the identity of the work, provisions are made for the adoption of preventive and repressive measures in the event of infringement of rights and resolve many other important issues.

8.4 THE BASIC PRINCIPLES OF COPYRIGHTS

Copyright is one of the most important intangible assets for any organization that owns them.

They are based on a basic principle, which is not linked to the way they are legally protected, but this has been the case over the years. It's the principle of *Exclusivity*. The copyright holder has the possibility to prohibit others from both the production and disposal of such goods.

We must pay attention to a number of specific issues at this point. The fact that we enshrine the copyright in a good and therefore we can only take advantage of it, does not mean that we automatically achieve our goals. The ability to produce revenue and profit is ultimately linked to the ways in which we implement our plans to enter new markets and place our products in them.

In order to be able to develop the products – goods of which we own the copyright, hard work is required. Legal protection is just the first step. Our market positioning, promotion, pricing, distribution and all that together, will prove whether we can finally have commercial success.

Finally, we must highlight one more thing. Whether it is a spiritual work or an object created by chance, e.g., a carved rock from seawater is something that has not yet been clarified either in its legal or substantive part. It is more related to one's personal relationship with art as a whole, than to the formal meaning of the term.

8.5 COPYRIGHTS & BUSINESS VALUE

Every business that holds an intellectual property has in its hands a hidden treasure. The ways and methods of action to exploit the treasure and transform it into income and profits are at its discretion. There is no doubt, however, that it is an important competitive advantage. It provides the following perspectives and capabilities:

- *Development through self-use exploitation, thus economic benefit, social recognition and improved market position,*
- *By licensing another person or business,*
- *Possibility of direct benefit through the sale of the intellectual right,*
- *Possibility of legal cover in case someone does not respect the intellectual right.*

8.6 RELATED RIGHTS

But it's not just the creators who have the rights. Behind each project there are several unsung workers and heroes, who have co-existed in many ways. Whether they have placed funds, large or small, or have adapted the projects, etc. These are called related rights. They are critical for the dissemination and reproduction of works, coexist with intellectual property rights, protection is also granted to them but is relatively limited.

For example, the following are considered holders of related rights:

- *Performers, actors, musicians, choirs and artists in general,*
- *Producers of phonograms or audiovisual works,*
- *Publishers of forms for their documentation and paging and*

- *Broadcasting organization.*

In short related rights are granted in parallel with intellectual property rights, are independent, do not affect it and can also function cumulatively.

8.7 PROTECTED DESIGNATIONS OF ORIGINS

In the context of the protection and development of intangible assets, we can't help but mention some excellent efforts that take place and give interesting characteristics to locally produced goods.

We are talking about characteristic indications on goods (food and drink for the most part) meaning 'Protected designation of origin'. This indication acknowledges a product produced in a specific region, or country and whose properties and specificities are due to the geographical environment where it was cultivated and developed. These products are created within a specific geographical area.

It is particularly important in this respect that this recognition grants intellectual property to the name not to the product and that protection is maintained indefinitely and is imposed by the authorities of each country.

8.8 DESIGNS & TEMPLATES

When we refer to the design, we mean the image of a product: its shape, outline and colors.

It's the external image, what one observes visually, that is. It is an important part of the good and results from the unique characteristics that distinguish it.

The border, lines, form, shape, and color are, among other things, characteristics of the external appearance of a product.

The exterior design of a product may be protected as such, provided that it has:

- *Unique character,*
- *Innovation, and*
- *Physical appearance that is not defined exclusively by its function.*

No one can overlook the fact that a legally protected design or template constitutes a significant competitive advantage and therefore an intangible asset for any business holding it.

9. IT INTANGIBLE ASSETS

9.1 INTRODUCTION TO IT APPLICATIONS

Intangible assets related to information technology (software, applications, databases, networks, IT systems), are now necessary for the organization of each company and even offer strategic advantages that no other organization can acquire without a large initial investment.

They are not discerned at first glance, but the dynamic they can develop is huge.

What do we call software? Software is a set of computer programs, together with instructions for use and licenses, that 'drive the hardware' of a computer to perform specific functions.

The term software is the opposite of the term 'hardware', which describes the physical layouts and interfaces necessary for the software to be installed and operated.

Software and, by extension, IT applications are an important intangible asset in today's economy of knowledge and technology. The development, possession, and operation of applications of all kinds, offers competitive advantages to the company that exploits them.

It is divided into the following categories:

- *System software*

When a group of software 'pieces' are designed and operated to control the physical side of a computer, they are called 'system software'.

The main part of a system software is the 'operating system'. The operating system is responsible for organizing the functions of a computer.

- *Programming software*

However, in order to create all kinds of software, the so-called 'programming languages' are used.

What is a programming language? It is a framework of rules designed to control and manage a computer through algorithms.

9.2 APPLICATION SOFTWARE

When a program is created to perform specific functions and meet special needs, it is called 'application software'.

Application software categories

An important intangible asset of particular characteristics and value is the 'application software'. The market it covers is not only large but also constantly growing. Every day new specialized application software programs are created for all kinds of business and operation.

According to a classic categorization, the application software is distinguished in:

- *Packed Software,* that is market-ready and covers the largest proportion of the market needs,
- *Custom Software,* developed on request, for individual applications with specific requirements.

A more detailed categorization of software may be as follows (indicatively):

- *special business functions,*
- *computer games or entertainment software,*
- *financial and accounting,*
- *enterprise resources planning (**ERP**),*
- *writing, correcting and managing content,*
- *educational software,*
- *special industrial software,*
- *applications and network management,*
- *safety and security,*
- *management of systems in general, etc.*

9.3 STATUS QUO OF THE SOFTWARE MARKET

Customer needs are growing in terms of software and application functions in general. So, software companies are also trying to meet these needs and everything consumers are asking for.

This process has led these organizations to a huge increase in the production of special software of all kinds.

The software market is divided into five (5) general categories, in which the separation is not always visible. However, we can give indicatively mention the following:

Category A: Business software

It is mainly installed in a few very large enterprises (mainly multinationals enterprises with a presence in many countries and with a global reach). These types of businesses need to cover complex processes.

Category B: Upper part of the software market

It is installed in large enterprises with difficulty in operations and processes. It is not usually active on a global scale but also has a presence in neighboring countries. So, it makes sense it has lower costs and there is a lot of competition developing in this market.

Category C: Medium software market

It is the big target market. This is where most application software manufacturers worldwide operate. Many companies that provide solutions to specific markets (vertical market approach) e.g., hotels, catering, construction, services, etc. have now appeared in this category.

Category D: Bottom of the software market

It is installed in small businesses. This type of software provides good and affordable solutions.

Category E: Introductory tier

It is the very cheap software and is aimed at small, usually sole proprietorships and freelancers. Offers solutions for working from home and is mostly single user.

9.4 DATABASE

A database is a collection of items that are organized to serve a specific purpose.

For example, on the computer we can keep the names and addresses of all our friends or customers. We may collect other data (e.g., historical data from an issue of interest to us) and organize it based on the date. We probably have many other files such as our balance sheets, or market data. Also, the files of the spreadsheet that are organized according to the uses as well as all the previous ones constitute a kind of database.

If we stand positively towards technology and like the use and exploitation of data, we can manage on our own by taking the necessary actions. In these cases, we are the administrators of the database.

However, what can be done when problems get bigger and bigger? What if we also have to share the input of data or the production of information with multiple people? This is the moment when a properly organized database is deemed necessary.

9.5 WHY WE USE DATABASES

But why is it necessary to use a database in a business? It is necessary because such a database collects data and is slowly being built. It aims to meet the needs of the departments of a company, usually leading to central control.

In addition, using a database, we have the following (indicatively):

- *Reduces application implementation time,*
- *Immediate availability of up-to-date information is supported,*
- *Data sharing between concurrent users is supported,*
- *There is more flexibility in the event of a change in requirements,*
- *Multiple aspects of the data are supported,*
- *Metadata storage is supported,*
- *Program independence is supported,*
- *Back-up is supported,*
- *Damage recovery procedures are supported,*
- *Complex associations between data are supported,*
- *Direct sales/purchase processing is supported,*
- *Unauthorized access is restricted,*
- *Many user interfaces are provided, etc.*

9.6 NETWORK SYSTEMS

Computers are no longer an asset for their material value and substance.

It is of particular interest to be able to connect to a network with many others at the same time, to provide increased power, give access to customers, suppliers, operators, databases, etc., elements necessary for the modern business.

Ensuring a functional and modern computer network makes every operation of a business easy to use and efficient.

It is an invisible treasure, which confers a comparative advantage on each organization.

9.7 INFORMATION SYSTEMS

Our daily lives are changing dramatically due to technological developments. Almost everyone now uses Smartphones for communication as well as increasingly sophisticated email systems and voice platforms. These kinds of technologies that have as their component the 'information', have dramatically changed the way people carry out their jobs and the way businesses are run.

Information technology refers to procedures, practices and systems that facilitate the processing and transfer of a significant amount of data. As the years go by, most of us, especially the new generation, become increasingly familiarized with the modern components of information technology.

An information system can be defined as a set of people, data, technology and organizational methods working together to collect, to process, to store and to transmit information in order to support decision-making.

Information systems are not just computers and processing. Information systems include employees who enter the data into them, the executives of the businesses carrying out staff - coordinating work but also the administration which studies the reports produced and the specific reports required each time.

An information management system supports the decision-making of business executives by producing standard, concise reports on a regular basis.

10. OPERATIONAL INTANGIBLE ASSETS

Operational intangible assets are perhaps the most important group for creating competitive advantages. It's a big chest, through which we haul high-value hidden treasures!

Such competitive advantages allow the company to generate exceptional value and profits. At the same time, they are also the determining factors that can influence critical decisions.

For example, there are cases of acquisitions or mergers, achieved at a significantly better price than that justified by the economic data, or even in a much shorter time, only because the target – business, possessed strategic and comparative advantages which were of great interest to the investor or led to synergies.

Below we analyze one by one the business intangible goods. They are worth studying!

- *Niche Marker*
- *Distribution channels*
- *Market shares*
- *Organization of the customer base*
- *E- business*
- *Procedures - processes*
- *Market research*
- *Research and development*
- *Technical knowledge & skills*

The possession of the above makes the business attractive to third parties and leads to the possession of strategic advantages, increasing both its turnover and profits.

10.1 NICHE MARKET

Definition

When we refer to a niche market, we mean a category of potential customers with specific characteristics and specific needs.

A niche market emerges when a segment of the large market is torn into smaller subsets, each of which has particular characteristics and for which we intend to meet these specific needs.

A niche market is interesting when potential customers are enough in multitude and obviously can afford to buy these special products or services that approach or cover their specificities.

In short, the establishment of a business with the aim of selling in a specialized market (Niche), allows us to take advantage of a part of the customers that has been overlooked by the large business that targets large-scale markets. Often such an effort becomes very successful as it focuses on a closed group with specific characteristics.

In some cases, entering such a special market may be the starting point for access to the largest - main market. If there is success within this special market, then we can add products or services. Due to the existence of a small but well-established customer base, growth in the main market can be achieved much faster than if the effort started from scratch.

The 'niche' strategy can be low cost (e.g., Airbnb small apartments in a large city) or differentiated (e.g., an expensive brand in travel cars e.g., for Taxi).

If there are buyers who want lower prices and can be satisfied, then the first strategy is excellent. If there are cases of consumers with a strong wallet and special needs, then the second strategy is great!

When a business successfully operates in a niche market, this does not necessarily mean that it will become competitive in the wider market. One does not necessarily ensure the other. But a dynamic business has potential and has to exhaust its capabilities.

Advantages & Disadvantages of a Niche Market

- What are the advantages of specialized businesses operating in a niche market?

  - *Less competition*. Given the targeting in a small - special market, the chances suggest that there is little to no competition. It is also much easier to connect to the main market when you are already specializing in one part of this market.
  - *Small budget.* With specialized marketing, we save large amounts of our budget. We do not waste money by sending, for example, leaflets to everyone, but instead we focus on the public - a specific objective. Advertising costs for specialised businesses are significantly lower.
  - *Loyal customers.* The customer is our king, and if he's happy, everything's positive! If customers love the special products or services offered and believe that they meet their expectations, then they will surely remain loyal!

But what are the disadvantages of specialized businesses?

- *Less growth potential*. Only a small part of the market will buy the products and therefore the profit margin and the total turnover may not be as large. If there is no expansion and growth based on the needs of the big market, products or services as well as growth, will encounter difficulties.

- *Facing the big shots*. After the small – specialized business is created and a good share of the narrow market is acquired, large companies will start to 'observe' this company. They may therefore try to integrate corresponding specific products – substitutes, into the large markets that already hold. So there's likely to be stiff competition from the big players.

10.2 ORGANIZATION OF THE CUSTOMER LISTS

Proper recording of the corporate customer list, as well as its organization and management, is vital, especially for small businesses.

The ability to keep a customer record with details (email, telephones, etc.), in any case increases the value and confers a competitive advantage because it helps to target the market, and to target as well continuous or partial approaches to offers, new products, wishes, bulk email – sms, etc.

The organization of a business's customer list is the largest asset of small businesses!

10.3 DISTRIBUTION CHANNELS

Purpose of the operational function of distribution

Depending on the market in which the company operates, the distribution channels of its products are also built. The aim in any case must be to meet the needs of the customer. In other words, it is the market's conditions that have the dominant role here.

The customer must be satisfied with his reasonable requirements. Where the product will arrive, in what condition and in how long the delivery will take place, is an obligation of the business. Under normal circumstances it tries to satisfy these three assumptions through the proper organization of distribution channels.

There are two important categorizations that make some businesses stand out for the proper functioning of the distribution process:

- The first is contact. But what do we mean by that? The organization of sales is essentially linked to the distribution channels. One company, one contact. This is the idea behind it. The entire operation of the business is at the customer's disposal in order to adequately meet his needs and in this effort distribution channels play a primary role.
- The second is implementation. Here we are talking about the execution of the order. And in order to make it come true, it is necessary to activate all available resources, so that the distribution channels deliver to the customer the right goods, in the correct condition and at the time of his choice.

The operating environment of distribution channels

The environment, in which the business operates, is the primary element of its organization. Its influence is the cornerstone of the way it works and should in no way be overlooked.

In this context, the development of distribution channels adds a key competitive advantage for any kind of business that has developed it and operates it in a meaningful way.

The proper organization and operation of distribution channels depends on many critical factors:

1) *Economic factors*. It is the demand that plays the dominant role in economic factors. Its change in the consumer environment, together with the provision of liquidity, is the catalysts for the financial soundness of customers.

2) *Topographical, climatic and infrastructure factors*. These conditions mainly concern transport infrastructure and the climatic conditions of each region.

3) *Demographic, social and educational factors*. The demography of each region, whether local or regional, is influenced by many factors. Dominant, however, appears to be the age distribution of the population (enlargement of the population or ageing) and the occupation of the inhabitants of the region (which confers prestige and entity).

4) *Members of the network*. Here we mainly mean suppliers who have the potential to influence either positively or negatively the operation of our distribution channels (e.g., if strategic orders are late etc.).

5) *Technological innovations*. The use of new innovative applications plays a big role in the customer's choices (electronic ordering process, modern sales processes using technologies, inventory management using computers, etc.).

6) *Competitors*. Competition is always a factor that should not escape our attention. As a business, we need to keep an eye on it, so that we can see changes in movements and directions. But we

must not fall into the trap of granting the initiative. We must not stand passive in the face of competition. We must constantly improve the operation of our business, remain the protagonists of developments. Customers reward it.

7) *Third-party support*. At this point we are talking about legal support for issues such as traffic regulations, shop opening hours, transport, etc., as well as information issues where cooperating businesses can provide us with specific market data.

Forms of distribution networks

Depending on how it operates, a business organizes the distribution channels it develops in two ways or a combination thereof. We are talking about direct distribution and indirect distribution.

We have direct distribution when there are no intermediaries. The business distributes the goods itself to its own employees, directly to customers without the mediation of a reseller.

We have indirect distribution when we use intermediaries to serve customers. Unlike direct distribution, indirect uses intermediate resellers and takes advantage of many levels of operation.

Direct and indirect distribution can be combined, and this is actually the most common type of operation. It's called multi-channel distribution. This type of operation is very interesting because it gives business options for customer service, depending on the factors that are important each time.

A business has the capability through multi-channel distribution to exploit the advantages of all forms, for its own benefit. For example, it can serve urban dwellers in the direct way and border area dwellers in the indirect way. With multi-room distribution the company has a variety of options in the ways of service and the benefits are not negligible.

Therefore, a distribution network usually operates in many forms, the most important are judged as follows:

- *The business may use exclusive agents and is therefore obliged not to designate anyone else in a specific geographical area. Even if a customer of this region addresses the business itself, it will refer him to the sole representative. If it also has representatives in many areas, everyone is obliged to sell the goods to customers only within their area.*

- *The business uses many free representatives, which are selected either because of quantitative factors (e.g., how many sales one commits to achieve), either with quality characteristics (e.g., local reputation, store location, etc.)*

A well-structured and organized distribution network is a valuable element for every business. It gives it a great competitive advantage.

Many third-party businesses put such organized companies on their radar. They are interested not only in closer cooperation but they also often proceed to mergers or acquisitions at a higher-than-normal price, if they are to exploit for their benefit a well-formed distribution network.

10.4 MARKET SHARE

Definition of market share

Market share represents the percentage acquired by a particular business, in relation to the total sales in a field during a specific period of time. In other words, it is a company's share of total sales in relation to the market in which it operates.

For example, if a company achieves a turnover of 10 million currency units annually at national level and the total number of the same products sold in that country is 200 million currency units, the company's market share in the country is 5%.

Market share can be a percentage of total sales in a city, region, country or continent. It can also be a percentage of the global market.Investors and analysts carefully monitor increases and decreases in market share, as this is an indication of the competitiveness of an organization's products or services.

As the overall market grows for a product, a company that maintains its market share will increase its revenues at the same rate. A company that grows its market share increases its revenue faster than its competitors. On the contrary, the loss of market share can indicate serious problems, which will require significant changes and possibly restructuring in many areas.

There are several ways in which a business expands its market share:

- *With price cuts,*
- *With use of commercials,*
- *With the introduction of new products & services,*
- *With the diversification of its the goods,*
- *With the attraction – approach of new market points, etc...*

Types of market share

There are several types of market share. Market shares may have value or volume. The market share in value as reported is based on a company's participation in the total sales of the field. Volume refers to the actual number of units sold by a company in relation to the total units sold on the market.

Market shares in value or volume do not always move in parallel. There is a possibility that the market share in value may be high and at the same time the volume share may be low.

In mass-consumption markets, where products are of low value or large quantity, comparing market share in value is the norm.

- *Market share in units*

They are the units (e.g., quantity in pieces) sold by a particular company as a percentage of total sales on the market, measured in the same units.

Market share in units (%) = 100 * Sales in units / Total sales in units.

- *Market share in revenue*

The market share in revenue differs from the market share in units, as it reflects the sale prices of the products. A simple way to calculate the relative price is to divide market share into income by market share into units.

Market share in revenue (%) = 100 * Sales revenue / Total sales market revenue.

For many economists, market share is not an intangible asset, but an economic phenomenon stemming from intangible fixed assets.

Either way, no matter how you consider them, the truth is that analysts radars constantly evaluate such data and thus make it attractive for a company with significant or even increasing market shares. They are a hidden treasure for every business!

10.5 E-BUSINESS

Why did e-business come into our lives so dynamically? What's the difference with e-commerce?

The world around us is changing, transforming. The internet is gaining thousands of people every day. Technological resistance is still going strong. Through the use of dynamic aspects of technology, business is constantly changing, promoting economic independence as an idea and an act.

This is The Electronic Business. It consists of two components, technological development and the will of entrepreneurs to develop!

It's different from e-commerce. By e-business we mean a package of activities supported by technology. On the contrary, e-commerce is just a small part of e-business. It's just the part where customers intersect with businesses.

E-business has now overwhelmed economic activity. Automated transactions carried out using technology and telecommunications are considered electronic business and indicatively we mention the following:

- *Electronic public services to other public entities, private sector businesses and ordinary citizens,*
- *Electronic advertising,*
- *Electronic payments,*
- *Electronic sales,*
- *Electronic orders,*
- *Electronic listings,*
- *Electronic updates and many other everyday applications...*

The ability of a business to participate dynamically, with innovation in e-business, offers an excellent competitive advantage!

10.6 PROCEDURES - PROCESSES

- *Procedures*

By operational process, we mean the recorded and structured step by step– actions (few or many), that must be followed within a business in order to arrive at the correct result of an event.

The 'event' mentioned above may relate to a customer, a market or part thereof, a supplier, an evaluation, a competition, an application to purchase infrastructure material, a job, etc.

Procedures in an association show organization and seriousness. Knowledge and experience do not remain in the minds of employees. They are recorded and made public. Thus anyone, new

or old cooperating with the company, has the opportunity to study and understand the sequence of actions that he must complete in order to reach the desired result.

The existence of procedures facilitates the corporate organization, the integration of a new employee into the human resources and corporate culture, as well as the control of the owner in any circumstances that will be deemed appropriate.

- *Processes*

By *operational process*, we mean the sequence of movements and actions of a person, in order to arrive at the desired result.

The operational processes are usually expressed with symbols, with the so-called flowcharts.

The flowchart consists of geometric shapes. Each of these shapes expresses a function or action.

They are a useful tool for studying, evaluating and improving recorded procedures as they highlight their evolution in an easy-to-understand way.

10.7 MARKET RESEARCH

Purpose of market research

Whether we're talking about a business in operation with an established market position, or about a start-up company, there's a tool that not only helps them, but is also deemed necessary for their development. This tool is market research.

A market survey can have a multitude of expressions. It helps a business to increase its sales, to maximize its profits, to increase its market share but, above all, to examine in detail the specific

characteristics it wishes to examine, in order to reveal those qualitative factors that can lead to maximizing its value.

Market research can be conducted by a business of any size, by startups, small, medium or large businesses. Its size and form does not matter as much as the targeting and dynamics it develops.

Through research of this nature, we can look for and study many qualitative data, such as:

- To analyze the demographic characteristics of a market in order to plan the actions required for each occasion,
- To highlight the corporate image that the consumer has, for the business unit,
- To design new products or services, that meet modern customers' requirements,
- To measure market growth dynamics,
- To examine the extent to which customer satisfaction is found, either from our products or overall in the market.
- Investigate whether an ad campaign can deliver the expected benefits and to what extent.

There are many factors that a market research may evaluate. It may seem like a contradiction at first sight, but it is an important asset for any business. Its elements can be desirable for many other organizations. For these reasons and provided that it is carried out systematically and correctly, it is considered an important intangible asset and offers great advantages.

Market research data

There are several different steps that we need to organize in order to arrive at a meaningful market research. For example, we can mention the following:

- Correct wording of the questions,
- Search for sources of information that will bring results,
- Selection of the points of purchase to be sampled,
- Collection of data,
- Extensive analysis of the data we collected and
- Presentation of these to the shareholders and the administration of the company.

Through the above steps, we come up with rational results for the market we are interested in.

Finally, market research is divided into quantitative and qualitative.

Quality research is carried out in subsets of the market that we are interested in. Through quality factors a business is essentially looking for the root causes, the relationships behind the numbers.

Qualitative research is carried out with a large number of participants. We usually look for numbers and percentages for products, consumers, market shares, and frequencies of customer choice and other issues of this kind.

The possession of specialized market research, the proper use of e-business, as well as structured procedures on the part of the company, are significant competitive advantages that add value and it would be good to highlight them at every opportunity!

10.8 RESEARCH & DEVELOPMENT

'R&D' essentially means Research & Development in business, with the aim of achieving innovations. Research and development as innovation tools, help people to evolve, improve their quality of life, go one step further each time.

In the modern business of increasing competition and constant change, the modernity that is being enjoyed through the R&D departments is the cornerstone of a company's success.

R&D departments should be made up of people with great creativity and ingenuity! For these reasons, the company that develops research and development within it, exudes dynamism and this does not go unnoticed!

10.9 TECHNICAL KNOWLEDGE & SKILLS

By referring to the term of 'Technical knowledge' we mean the process of learning specific technical information or a technical object. It consists of a theoretical approach and practice, a specific work related to technical issues.

The knowledge and skills developed, as well as the experience accumulated on specific 'technical issues', are certainly a comparative advantage for the company that exploits them.

Example: The process of finding raw materials (mechanisms, circuits, tools, etc.) and assembling them to produce a product e.g., a machine or robot, performing a specific technical function.

Special Technical Knowledge = Intangible element that offers enormous value to a business.

11. COOPERATIVE INTANGIBLE ASSETS

Every modern company is interested in the development of partnerships and relationships with its 'environment', i.e., with customers, suppliers, consumers, the wider society etc.

This group of intangible assets is an important factor in the success of each organization. It consists of the following elements:

- *Positive business image*
- *Business culture*
- *Corporate partnerships*
- *Customer Organization & Administration*
- *Supplier evaluation*
- *External collaborations*

The above aspects seek to reflect the operation of the business in relation to the overall partnerships it develops. It must set specific objectives and satisfy them in order to improve its economic and quality performance.

Partnerships always grow behind numbers. They are resolutely affected, and that is why we must preserve them with great care.

11.1 POSITIVE BUSINESS IMAGE

The creation of the business image, i.e., the 'outward' corporate expression, is a primary intangible good. It is an important collaborative phenomenon and its contribution to corporate value is undeniable.

A classic example of creating a 'positive image' is the 'Corporate Social Responsibility' through which vital business moves is

highlighted that aim to raise awareness of social issues, environmental issues, etc.

It offers the following:

- *Has a positive impact on the consumers*

A socially responsible company cares enough about its impact on society and not just on profit. By creating activities that promote the well-being of all citizens and the environment, it contributes to achieving positive change.

- *Creates a positive business image and better recognition*

Organizations that promote strong and consistent initiatives gain more popularity and recognition from consumers than those that do not.

- *Builds trust and strengthens corporate partnerships*

Customers, suppliers, employees and generally partners of a company feel empowered when involved in events that are worth taking care of passionately.

- *Encourages business growth*

Employees who are actively involved in positive activities have increased creativity, which in turn inspires new development efforts for products, services and corporate systems.

Examples of developing a good business image: Press releases, telephone service lines (low cost or even free), corporate sponsorships, public information campaigns, etc.

11.2 BUSINESS CULTURE

When we refer to a set of rules of conduct within a company, but which follow a 'merit system', then we are talking about the 'business culture'.

It is directly affected by the following factors:

- *the organization of the business,*
- *the particular elements of its potential,*
- *The code of conduct it has developed.*

Business culture can best be described as «the way we work here».

It consists of hierarchy and respect for the system of values that everyone accepts, whether they are employees or ordinary partners of the company.

A strong business culture develops a great strategic advantage over competition, mainly because it expresses a structured philosophy of management on which you can rely.

To a large extent, the business culture is created by the values of its founders and continues from administration to administration.

11.3 CORPORATE PARTNERSHIPS

If a business participates in a cluster (cooperative formation) or holds a dominant position in a market, it creates great comparative advantages and all this is reflected in its value.

The interdependence of oligopolistic enterprises can take the form of 'collusion'.

If a product or service has no substitutes and a business is the only one offering it, then that organization is considered a monopoly.

11.4 CUSTOMER ORGANIZATION & MANAGEMENT

Introduction

Without this cooperative intangible asset and economic phenomenon, the legal entity does not exist. If it grows, however, the business becomes sought after!

In the modern economic situation, where competition is becoming more and more intense, companies are looking for different, more modern and efficient market approaches than traditional models.

Customers are now more demanding, stronger, more selective and with greater purchasing power. It is very difficult to manage them.

In order for the businesses to cope satisfactorily with the above issue, they redefine the methods of communication with their customers but also their own corporate structures.

Value creation is the foundation of entrepreneurship now. From the simple worker in the packaging of the product, to the manager of marketing, a little of value needs to be added, in order to improve the organization of sales and satisfy the needs of customers. Companies, with their daily effort, manage all their customers and further develop their trading relationships, with the aim of creating accumulated value in their transactions.

What are important – strategic customers.

What do we mean by 'strategic customers'? They are the large customers of a company, who prepare frequent orders and large in quantity, volume and value.

Strategic customers are the most important ones for any business. They must be treated as a 'crown jewel'! 'Big customers' are one of the most valuable assets of any business! If they are lost, in addition to strengthening competition, there will also be immediate difficulties in the corporate operation.

Usually, such strategic clients have large and specialized requirements. They want special treatment and immediate response to their orders. Businesses in order to cover them use special 'sellers', who usually have a lot of experience in customer management (Key Account Managers). Using CRM systems helps Key Account Managers serve large customers and aims to solve problems usually before they even occur.

11.5 SUPPLIER EVALUATION

Supplier selection & evaluation criteria

An important chapter for each business is the supplier. Proper supply of raw materials, commodities and goods in general is of paramount importance and should in no case be overlooked...

Each serious company selects suppliers with the aim of a stable cooperation for a long period of time.

The previous analytical examination of suppliers, their financial data, their historical course, the dynamics they develop, the ways of supply, etc. are the guarantees for a proper cooperation. These are the ones that shield the business and maximize the value of this intangible good. It is therefore extremely necessary to establish criteria for the evaluation and selection of suppliers.

Being important links in the chain, quite often they are the same people who express an interest in cooperation. But the usual thing is for the company itself to look for them. The cost-benefit relationship almost always starts at the purchase price and this is the obvious thing to happen. However, the evaluation should also proceed to other factors such as:

1. Administration cooperation

This is an extremely important factor because it is the supplier's administration that makes the decisions. The ability to agree with it and the compliance with the agreements directly affect the cooperation relationship.

2. Employee skills

This category examines the capabilities of the Supplier's employees as a whole (excluding management, i.e.). This criterion should not be underestimated because the education and training of other staff give clear advantages.

3. Technical Know-how

Producing a product is not an easy task. The technical characteristics must be able to be implemented by the supplier so that the product has the necessary information, during the whole implementation.

4. Quality

Very important criterion because **quality** systems (ISOs, etc.), various certificates, corporate structure, etc. must examined.

5. Respect for the environment

No one wants to be involved in working with company suppliers of 'bad social image'.

6. Financial stability

The supplier's cooperation with banks and investors plays an important role, because it solves any liquidity problems and does not create obstacles to production.

7. Long-term cooperation

In recent years, the intention and commitment to long-term relationships has been increasingly positively assessed.

In addition to the above, very important and widely used criteria in the evaluation and selection of suppliers are seriousness, commitment to quality, reliability, improvement that can be demonstrated as no one is perfect, pricing procedures, robustness as well as issues such as responsiveness, cooperation, professionalism, moral values, trust etc.

11.6 EXTERNAL COLLABORATIONS

Companies should be able to cooperate perfectly with their external partners (accountants, economists, lawyers, etc.).

Successful cooperation with external partners is a skill and therefore an intangible economic phenomenon of great value.

It enables the business to pursue business opportunities and take risks with great flexibility.

The external partner does not charge the business a fixed, but a variable cost. This offers flexibility and in many projects this is necessary.

As a theoretical approach it is correct, because in addition to the special needs served by such a partner e.g., training in sales service or special services, it can and should meet a wide range of operational requirements.

An external partner in a business can very often, offer an angle of assessment of issues, outside the system of corporate everyday life, i.e., from the routine of the same way of working, that even if it is successful, over time it declines in efficiency.

12. FINANCIAL INTANGIBLE ASSETS

Financial intangible assets are already well known. By their very nature, the possibility of exploiting those, leads to great strategic advantages for any business that owns them.

12.1 ROYALTIES

Royalties are the contractual obligation to use assets such as patents, copyrights, franchises, special privileges or natural resources. It is not a lump sum but a percentage of the revenue from the use of this right.

The royalties are paid by the 'tenant' of the intangible assets to the person who has established the legal rights.

Royalties reflect the continuing right of the franchisee (tenant) to use the franchisor system and the 'brand' (owner of the right).

12.2 LEASING

What does leasing mean? Let's set an example. A company chooses to invest for its operational needs in a property, some production machinery, cars or printers etc. Instead of buying what the business needs itself, it comes to an agreement with the leasing company which buys the specific items and rents them to the business, taking in return the so-called 'rents'.

The benefit of this financial move is that the business spends its capital while not increasing its borrowing. In addition, the leasing company's purchase of these items helps not to waste money on resources unrelated to actual operational needs.

Leasing is an important financial intangible asset.

It can be used by enterprises of all kinds and sizes, from sole proprietorship to multinational!

12.3 COMMERCIAL LEASES

The amount of the lease, its duration, the possibility of subletting, as well as other conditions in a rental room, greatly affect the fixed costs of each business as well as the 'flexibility' it can present.

Any lease term which may favor the business either financially or operationally, confers the business an undeniable comparative advantage.

Every businessman has to monitor the rent, as a percentage of his turnover and profits, in order to control his competitiveness.

12.4 FINANCIAL RELATIONS

Financial relations are an important intangible economic phenomenon. When the company wishes or is obliged to restructure (e.g., its lending), or after crises for which the company is not responsible but suffers the consequences (e.g., Covid-19 crisis), the favorable relations with investors, financial institutions, venture capital, fund etc. offer the company this possibility!

Businesses that move away from the investment society, unfortunately reduce response opportunities when things start to go wrong (crises, falling sales, profits, emergencies, etc.).

12.5 VALUE OF SIGNED CONTRACTS PENDING EXECUTION

The term '*value of signed contracts pending execution*' means valid agreements that have already been contracted but are still unfulfilled.

For example, a construction company has contracts with large projects under way, or also a commercial business has a special agreement with a large – strategic customer for the delivery of a significant number of products (and therefore high turnover) within the next year.

However, there is always the possibility that something will go wrong and the agreements will be cancelled or not valid as originally agreed, however, with the appropriate handling, this risk can be reduced.

13. ANTHROPOCENTRIC INTANGIBLE ASSETS

The skills, skillfulness and knowledge that is already possessed and constantly evolved by the employees within a company, is briefly called 'Human Capital'.

Intangible assets play a key role in legal entities. Understanding the importance of anthropocentric intangible assets, the intangible phenomena they create, as well as the formulation of the appropriate political administration of the human factor, contributes to the creation of competitive advantages of significant value.

No matter how much the development of technology evolves, no matter how much telecommunications are developed, no matter how far ahead artificial intelligence or software goes, human knowledge and experience will be the pillar, the basis for business efforts.

Moreover, an economy operating in the modern globalized economic environment cannot be developed only with unskilled workers and on the basis of a low minimum wage. To move forward it also needs skilled, educated workers.

It is clear that human resources are the most important capital in a business. It is the catalyst for success. It links innovation with productivity and corporate development, the important growth factors.

Training, specialization and incentives to improve the position of executives within corporate structures are also factors of success.

Business leadership is intertwined with the creation of talent and the exploitation of these by businesses. These relationships strengthen the overall corporate commitment to education through cooperation with universities and executive training schools.

The benefits of using human capital are summarized as follows:

- *Employee loyalty,*
- *Attracting qualified, talented staff and*
- *Optimization of the level of operation by increasing productivity.*

With all of the above, each business acquires a very important success factor.

13.1 HUMAN RESOURCES CONTRACT

Contracts & engagement with specialized industry executives = Competitive advantage!

The rewards sought by an employee are the driving force behind his performance and directly affect the satisfaction he gains from his work and, in effect, its quality.

Favorable contracts and special additional benefits signed by a business with 'skilled executives in its field' constitute a comparative advantage for it and as such an intangible asset of exceptional value.

13.2 PROFESSIONAL QUALIFICATIONS

Professional qualifications: Wide scope (administration, computer use, decoration, engineering and more).

Professional qualifications are based on the knowledge and experience available to the employee, which he uses through his work.

Professional skills are acquired for life through experience and perception. They help the employee to highlight the knowledge and skills he has acquired, so he can perform a task correctly and with responsibility.

The competence of an executive is developed through the acquisition of professional qualifications, which are indicative of:

a. Knowledge and what we call 'education',
b. Specializations acquired (training),
c. The use of technology and telecommunications,
d. The seriousness
e. The interest in evolution for both himself and the company.

13.3 CORPORATE TRAINING - GUIDANCE

Employees attend seminars, train and improve on specific fields of knowledge. The training is organized by the business itself, or from external sources (from associations, educational companies, other entities, etc.). The proper organization of such events and the attitude of workers towards them determine their degree of success.

The corporate training of executives should aim at:

- *increasing knowledge,*
- *improving teamwork,*
- *dealing with changes or crises in the operation,*
- *staff development.*

The corporate training process in the broadest sense is designed to provide knowledge and information to employees of businesses, not only for reasons of general education but also for reasons of improvement in specific issues such as dilemmas, difficulties in decision making, crises, negotiations, etc.

The ability to train is a major factor in the dynamic development and growth of the whole business.

It is an important intangible and offers long-term competitive advantages that should not in any way be underestimated.

13.4 LEADERSHIP

Are you born a leader or are you made into one? Many consider leadership to be a series of acquired characteristics that man carries inherently. Others believe that the leader is sculpted through the obstacles, difficulties and issues he faces in his working life.

The truth is somewhere in between. The leader needs both the right character and the necessary experience to be able to inspire the team that follows him.

If within coexistence in a working group, everyone follows the dictates of his character, shows respect, is a team player and there is a common goal, the real leader will emerge on his own.

13.5 INTERNAL CORPORATE COMMUNICATION

Good internal communication in business = dissemination and continuation of knowledge and experience.

Good internal communication, i.e., the development of a relationship of mutual trust between the employees of a company, is the cornerstone for building an atmosphere of cooperation, understanding of corporate objectives and motivation for everyone to achieve the common goal.

It is worth noting that the control of internal communication is particularly important. Management must be aware of any

situations of non-creative internal communication in order to be able to deal immediately with such issues. There are cases where actions to improve climate and cooperation are needed. After all, prevention is better than treatment. Direct feedback of positive attitude and proper internal communication from all through an objective and confidential mechanism, can make it particularly productive.

13.6 PROFESSIONALISM - INTEGRITY

PROFESSIONALISM:

The good quality and the effective working methods, through which one starts and completes one's work.

INTEGRITY:

Avoiding any kind of offence, professional or scientific.

13.7 GENERAL EDUCATION

When we mention the concept of 'General Education' we mean the formal education that citizens acquire from a school mainly at a young age.

Education does not offer specific vocational training to the individual. It is essentially the foundation, on which everyone will be able to build their professional and personal path.

For example, lessons related to general education are history, geography, geometry, mathematics, chemistry, physics, literature, art, music, etc.

13.8 TECHNICAL KNOW - HOW

Know How refers to a specific 'special' knowledge and expertise, that an employee acquires mainly through his experience and his professional career.

It is not possible for any form of knowledge to be imprinted and described by a machine. That's why know-how will always be a personal specialization and therefore an anthropocentric intangible asset.

Examples of know-how reference can be mentioned: '*how we sell over the internet*' as well as the phrase '*what is the true taste of an aged bottle of whisky*'!

14. PRIVILEDGED INTANGIBLE ASSETS

14.1 STATE LICENSES

By 'state license' we mean the approvals given by the state (government, ministries, municipalities, state entities) to a company.

The purpose for the organization that uses them, is to do so freely by cooperating with the state and with goverment assistance and relief, so that in the end it does not take illegal actions.

Examples of Licenses:

- *Licenses to operate radio or television stations,*
- *mineral extraction licenses,*
- *casino operation,*
- *rights to use state ports,*
- *import licenses, etc.,*

Most of the time 'licenses' are provided by government entities and are non-transferable.

The 'license' for the 'production and exploitation', effectively guarantees freedom to its holder to exercise the rights offered to him.

14.2 FAVORABLE CONTRACTS

By contracts, we mean agreements (usually written but also oral on a case-by-case basis) between two parties.

The usual practice in a contract is as follows: One side (which may be a legal or natural person) carries out the actions agreed in accordance with contractual obligations and the other side receives the pre-agreed remuneration. A particularly favorable price achieved under special circumstances, contracts offering special privileges, etc. are a clear competitive advantage for the businesses that own them.

14.3 REAL OPTIONS

Real Options, or preference rights, express in today's economic reality a very important effort to highlight business value. Preference rights are goods that exist within many businesses worldwide but have not yet been exploited as they should be.

They are essentially great investment opportunities. They relate to inactive intangible assets, which, if used in the future, will generate significant revenues.

'Right of preference' for example is the possession of a software application or information system, used only within a business when it could be sold or rented, generating large revenues and generating positive or even increasing cash flow.

Also, Real Option is the possession of a non-exploitable patent. If its practical exploitation is initiated, it will help generate revenue and thus create additional value for its shareholders.

Real Options: Future exploitation of non-functional intangible assets

From all of the above, the contribution of intangible assets and the economic phenomena produced by them, is demonstrated and clearly visible for the creation of a competitive advantage and thus the preservation of the business at a high level of competition.

It's the hidden treasures that if we take advantage of them, we'll increase corporate value!

15. VALUATION OF INTANGIBLE ASSETS

Introduction

How is the concept of valuation meant, as science or as an art?

It's Science because it combines quantitative data, the mechanics of the application of methods, the pure perspective of the technocrat...

It's Art because it needs the creativity of quality data, the technique of assessments, the sensor of danger, of risk, of decisions...

The word 'Valuation' whenever mentioned brings to mind concepts purely economic (price, cost, value etc.) It is therefore reasonable to believe that any assessment will start with financial agents, business advisory firms, large financial institutions, etc.

With regard to intangible assets due to their characteristic invisibility, it can also be assumed that the attempt to quantify them, may have been initiated by advertising companies, marketing departments of organizations, etc.

In the present case, the attempt to assess intangible assets was initiated by both of the abovementioned parties. The need to express a value for an intangible asset or a group of them is shared by both economists and marketing executives.

The importance of intangible assets is not only very signific but also constantly increasing. Once their value was considered small, so there was no particular reason to start a process of assessing them. In today's economic reality, however, intangible assets are of considerable value and the debate about their expression in the financial statements has flared up.

In this light, attempts to evaluate brands, copyrights, patents, software applications were born, but also in general the goodwill they generate in the valuations of the businesses that own and exploit them.

At first, as was logical, mainly financial methods were developed. Over time, however, and due to the nature of intangible assets, methods have emerged that also reflect the qualitative characteristics. These are more related to consumer behaviors and other qualitative data and factors that are quite interesting and we will study them along the way.

The methods of assessing the value of intangible assets are divided into two (2) large groups:

A) The Financial valuation models and
B) The Quality valuation models.

We then present the most important methods of these two large groups. Before going into detail, however, it would be a good thing to study the definitions of so-called 'values'.

15.1 DEFINITIONS OF VALUES

When we start the discussion on the valuation of intangible assets, we need to understand the context of our discussion, the terms of the game, that is to say.

What kind of value are we exactly talking about? What is our need and what do we want to achieve? In short, what is the purpose of the valuation?

There are four (4) basic definitions for values. With the following categorization we will try to unravel the concepts:

1. **Market value**: It is interpreted if by comparing the value of some similar intangible assets in a market, we discover the average. The valuation of the intangible we are looking for will be close to this value.
2. **Fair value**: It means that there is a positive desire and the willingness to achieve the transaction, both from the seller's point of view and from the buyer's point of view. Both come into direct negotiations with each other and seek the common factor.
3. **Owner value**: It is the price that the owner of the intangible asset wishes to achieve in order to accept its sale and the loss of the benefits offered to him.
4. **Tax value**: It is directly related to the value as derived from the legislation of each State and the tax obligations that are arising.

15.2 FINANCIAL VALUATION MODELS

It is obvious that in the field of business we should be able to measure something when we want to run it, make use of it and take advantage of it. Let alone if we're talking about intangible assets. Without measurement we cannot understand the leverage that develops between our actions and the value.

The valuation methods of intangible assets, which have been reported from time to time to date, are almost fifty (50) and more!

No method is perfect. No one can meet all of our needs. In the end, it all depends on the purpose for which we wish to devise the valuation and, of course, on the nature of the intangible asset. However, the process of using more than one method offers some kind of security. It helps us observe the intangible asset from many angles, so we get a clear picture of its potential.

The three (3) most representative financial methods for the valuation of intangible assets are as follows:

Comparable method.
The value of intangible assets is calculated compared to corresponding recent market transactions.

Cost methods.
Intangible fixed assets are valued in relation to their development costs. Here the historical cost data is essential.

Income methods.
These methods analyses the future cash flows of the company (economic benefit) derived from the exploitation of the intangible assets.

15.2.1 Comparable Method

The comparable method assesses the intangible assets of interest to us by investigating all transactions carried out in the recent past, in relation to similar characteristic intangible goods.

This method is often found mainly in the Real Estate market. It is theoretically an excellent valuation method because values can be directly determined by market data. So, what's better than this?

The problem with this method is that comparable transactions are relatively rare. In general, there is no plethora of transactions or 'typical markets' (e.g., stock exchange of intangible assets) in order to obtain data. Acquisitions of intangible assets are not a rule that is often repeated.

Most intangible assets are created not to be sold but to be exploited. So, most companies keep them and they don't aim to sell them.

Nor should it be overlooked that 'uniqueness' is an interwoven concept with that of intangible assets. It is very difficult to find a corresponding intangible element similar to the one that needs to be assessed.

But even if data is found, the comparison is not simple. It is very difficult to find similar recent transactions on specific intangible assets. The special nature of intangible assets often leads the investor to evaluate their acquisition with his own corporate characteristics (e.g., synergies at the operational level that we don't know or by not knowing details we cannot understand). So in such cases, values beyond reason may appear for us and our corporate needs.

Moreover, it is common for acquisitions of intangible assets, even when they occur, to be only a relatively small part of a larger commercial transaction. In fact, in most cases the details of these deals are not announced.

In conclusion, while the comparable method for the valuation of one or more intangible assets seems ideal at the theoretical level, it cannot often be effectively implemented.

In fact, if, in addition to the above-mentioned factors, we also take into account other factors affecting all types of transactions such as e.g., economic cycles, periods of intense acquisition and merge activity, specific incentives or bargaining power, etc., then we see that the valuation of intangible assets is very difficult to achieve by the comparable method.

An exception confirming the rule may be considered to be the name of a business or otherwise the brand name.

Brand names are an intangible asset that often appears on the balance sheets of large and very large enterprises (usually multinationals). This gives us a significant amount of data so that we can make comparisons with our own brand.

For brands, therefore, because of their specificities, we believe that the comparable method should be included in the valuation methods we use to estimate its value.

15.2.2 Cost-Based Approach

The method of valuation of intangible assets on the basis of cost is quite important. Its purpose is to assess the future benefits of the possession of intangible assets, in relation to the costs of these at all points of their creation.

Examples include research and development costs, labor costs (fees, bonuses, allowances), general costs (taxes, various or even exceptional costs, etc.), the costs of displaying and advertising the specific property, any investments for improvements, etc. The cost

method is almost always in line with the accounting approach in force in each country according to the legislation in the specific subject.

Clarifying, therefore, the cost method attempts to value intangible assets, calculating the money spent on the creation of the intangible asset in its current form.

The conservativeness of the method is highlighted by the fact of the conflict between two major professional groups. Accountants and advertisers. Because it offers zero information about the future, it is considered a conservative method but accountants treat it as the most acceptable. On the other hand, the advertising and marketing industry does not give it much weight precisely for the reasons mentioned above. It does not take into account the added value that a structured and lasting advertising campaign can create.

As a method it is simple to use, so it has several followers. It can be used and studied without requiring a lot of staff and is prepared at a fast pace giving immediate effect.

Difficulties arise in cases where the cost is not net, so it cannot be accurately distributed. In these cases, which are common, the allocation of costs must be done correctly so the intangible asset valued at that time will not be overburdened. The issue here is not so much the direct cost which can be easily found, but any indirect costs which, in order to be properly exploited, spadework is necessary for the operational work. When the intangible asset has been exploited by a business for a long period of time, the point at which the distribution of costs should start, is often indistinguishable.

In fact, once the cost-gathering process is complete, it is up to us to decide the interest rate through which the flows of the past will have the 'the right value' in the present. For example, a cost three years ago is of greater value today, on the basis that if we had this money available it would now have more value because of inflation.

The cost-based valuation method is differentiated into the following two sub-cases:

- *The sub-method of cost recovery and*
- *The cost replacement sub-method.*

The negative aspect of the cost method as a whole is that it sees only the past and not the future. But long-term investments, such as intangible assets, yield over time and not directly. So often the costs increase without showing the benefits. These will appear after years...

The cost method can also falsify the valuation by applicable legislation and tax arrangements by country. These have the potential to distort value by underestimating or overestimating the valued intangible asset.

In addition, an advertising campaign offers recognition to the business and intangible asset (e.g., a brand) by building the brand of the future. This cannot be reflected in most cases.

Finally, the cost method in the valuation of an intangible asset does not take into account the opportunity cost at all. The money invested could be used by the company in another field. Of course, no one lives in the present and the future alternately, but very often managers can intuitively decide whether another solution would be more advantageous or not.

By further analyzing the two sub-methods of cost we have important data which are remarkable.

Cost Recovery Method

Through the historical flashback and examination of the costs of the past to find the cost of an intangible asset, the method of 'recovery' gives significant results. According to this method, the value of the intangible asset is equal to the total historical cost of 'creating it', discounted of course to the present.

The 'cost recovery' effort is considered quite simple and is often used. However, in some cases it is not at all easy to go back to the past in order to calculate the total cost in detail.

Intangible assets such as research and development-based projects, software application investments, databases, etc., have expenditure that can be easily identified. So, the method of recovery finds fertile ground.

The method is reinforced by the fact that in the past the costs were less complex (e.g., Ads were minimal) and therefore it is easier to identify the costs.

Ultimately, cost recovery as a method of valuation of an intangible asset is relatively simple to use, but does not offer information on future developments.

Replacement Cost Method

Unlike the 'recovery' method, the 'replacement cost' method sees the creation of the intangible asset from an alternative perspective.

'Replacement cost' tries to find out the cost of 'recreating' the item. It is an important alternative approach, but it is highly subjective in the process of redefining expenditure.

It takes into account the investments and costs necessary to 'replace' this intangible element with a new one but of the same usefulness. This excludes so-called 'outdated' intangible assets.

In general, the method of 'replacement cost' or otherwise 'reconstruction', does not have the disadvantages of the recovery method, but is a more laborious process, with a significant degree of subjectivity and the possibility of influencing the data that will be taken into account by the assessor.

15.2.3 Income-Based Approach

If there is a method of valuation of intangible assets, which they consider to be their 'property' and is used commonly by economists, it is this one. In general, it is one of the most commonly used methods.

The income method matches the value of the intangible asset with the current value of its future economic benefits.

When we talk about 'future economic benefit' in a business, we mean increasing turnover, increasing profits, reducing costs, any investments that are needed and generally anything that offers to optimize its financial data and of course relates to future money flows.

If we are talking about an intangible asset, the method of income is formed through forecasts of future benefits (in turnover, profits, etc.) that it will offer to a business.

But when we talk about future flows, i.e., predictions of economic benefits from an intangible asset, there is certainly uncertainty. This uncertainty needs to be quantified in some way.

What's the danger here? It is the possibility that they will not achieve the predictions that have been devised. How is uncertainty quantified, i.e., risk? Through the discount factor. This rate is nothing more than the interest rate, i.e., a figure through which we discount future economic benefits in the present.

In other words, this number (the discount rate) represents the risk and shows us at the end, how much future forecasts are worth at today's prices (i.e., the economic benefits we expect from the intangible asset).

What will be the percentage we will receive as a risk interest rate is related to the investor, the nature of the intangible asset, the market, the economic cycle and other factors which are of a technical nature and do not need more analysis at present.

Another factor that plays an important role in the income method is the time benefit of the intangible asset we value. Here we mean how long the period of economic benefits we foresee will last.

There are intangible assets with a specific time horizon (e.g., a contract with a customer or supplier). In the event of its valuation, the provisions should cease in the year in which this contract expires. Contrastingly, in another intangible element (e.g., in a brand) there is no specific time-out and therefore the economic benefits can be predicted ad infinitum.

From all this we understand the care through which the analyst must quantify the future value of the intangible asset. Its useful life is influenced by a number of factors (natural, technological, legal, etc.) which must be at the heart of the calculation of its lifespan.

Using the income method, therefore, all future benefits must be defined for the period of time necessary and influenced by the factors mentioned above.

Let us set an example again. If we wish to value a copyright, we estimate the duration of its usefulness ad infinitum (as such rights have a time horizon of up to 70 years from the death of the author). On the contrary, if we are talking about another intangible asset such as a mobile software application, it can only have a useful life of three or four years...

The duration factor is dominant in the income method for the reasons mentioned above. As appraisers we have to monitor it because it affects value to a superlative degree.

The reader of this chapter can feel that he is in deep water. But this isn't the case. The data listed concern specialized business consultants and experienced assessors who deal specifically with such issues. Besides, a valuation isn't just science. You do not place numbers and the final result is automatically generated. A value-appreciation study is also an art. A lot of scientific knowledge needs to be combined, and sometimes a different approach, in order to evaluate the data. For this reason, the assessor must have sufficient knowledge and experience.

Price - Remuneration Method

The income method also applies to brands. In fact, due to their specificity as an intangible asset, the following analysis is interesting.

We present the price - remuneration sub-method. The core of this method is the existence of known and unknown labels on a product or group of products (i.e., one product group with a specific brand

and wide range of advertising and another group of corresponding products but anonymous, without a known brand).

The value of the brand is calculated by the difference in the price of the branded product in relation to the anonymous product and multiplying it by the total volume of branded sales.

The method of remuneration - price considers that the brand in a group of goods, creates an additional benefit for customers - consumers. This benefit is the extra amount they are willing to pay to obtain this branded product.

This discrepancy between the prices of a branded product and an anonymous product, is for this method the difference that adds the brand name to the good.

15.3 QUALITY VALUATION MODELS

Methods of measuring the value of intangible assets do not stop at financial models. They go further by applying multidimensional quality models and which are synthesized through a fermentation between less accounting and more behavioral models. However, they are divided into three (3) main categories:

Market capitalization methods

Market capitalization methods assess the value of intangible assets through the data in the official financial statements.

They measure intangible assets as a whole, paying attention to the difference between book value and market value in a business.

These methods distinguish the difference between the capitalization of the shares and the market corporate value and highlight it, as the total value in the intangible goods of the organization.

Return on assets methods

Asset efficiency methods refer to the return on intangible assets offered to the business, valuing them at an overall level.

This method approaches the performance of intangible assets in many ways producing an overall value, but always as its basis is the measurement of the performance of the enterprise as a whole.

Quality indicators

Quality indicator methods analyze intangible asset data by calculating significant corporate quality characteristics. With the methods of quality indicators, we do not obtain monetary value as a result, but indicators, tables and graphs.

The aim is to highlight those qualitative factors that make up and ultimately decisively influence the development and course of intangible assets in an enterprise, whether positive or negative.

15.3.1 Market capitalization methods

Market to Book Value

The Market to Book value method is quite simple to capture and very widespread in the market. It does not present any particular difficulties in its calculation, but it also faces several opponents. It is expressed by the formula:

Intangible business assets (Intellectual capital) = Market value / Book value).

If the index is a number greater than one (>1) then the company has intangible assets that are not shown in the official financial statements. If the index is less than one unit (<1), the corporate liabilities that are likely to be linked to intangible assets exceed its intellectual capital.

As a method it initially seems easy to produce, but presents difficulties mainly in its interpretation. The core of its theoretical approach is that at the 'market value' the extra material assets are intangible. The 'book value' is essentially the funds of the business itself as shown in the balance sheet.

The ease of its conception is offset by the fact that it does not take into account a number of important factors which may affect the value of intangible assets. These factors may be future cash flows to and from the company, technological developments, new capital, etc.

Another negative point of this method is that the denominator of the index reflects events of the past, while the market value is also shaped by future expectations. So, this is where an important practical inconsistency emerges.

The accounting approach is also significantly influenced by legal arrangements which sometimes significantly affect it. So, results may appear very different from reality. The book value is also affected by costs, taxation and other factors not related to intellectual capital.

In conclusion, the 'Market to Book value' method is simple as an idea, but cannot give the most reliable results. It is usable if we use

it in combination with other methods of valuation of intangible assets.

Tobin's Q

The 'Tobin's Q' method is an evolution of 'market to book value' method. It is an important development, in the process of measuring intellectual capital. It was named after the homonymous economist 'James Tobin'. This method is known by the mention of the letter 'Q'. At first it was used for investment decisions but its general usefulness quickly became clear.

Also, the index 'Tobin's Q' has the same numerator as the 'Market to book value' method, i.e., the Market Value. The difference lies in the denominator. There it does not calculate the book value (equity), but the cost of replacing the company's assets (fixed assets including long-term financial assets). The formula expressing the method is:

Intangible business assets = Market value / replacement cost).

And here, if the index shows as a result of a measurement more than one (>1) then it is considered that the company has significant intangible assets and therefore has comparative advantages over its competitors. The method assumes that this difference is due to its intellectual capital.

If the company is listed on a stock market, then as a market value we can obtain its stock market value.

Usually in enterprises with high intellectual capital (property), high technology and knowledge creation, a greater 'Q' is verified than in enterprises with less intellectual capital.

Despite the fact that the 'Q' index gives modernity to the valuation of intellectual capital in relation to the Market to Book value method, it is not simple. Trying to determine the cost of replacing assets in a business is easy to say but difficult to implement.

However, the 'Q' indicator gives us an important indication of the dynamics of the business and we need to evaluate it. It also acquires particular value in the comparison process of undertakings belonging to and operating in the same market, as well as in monitoring the development of total intellectual capital in an organization.

15.3.2 Return on assets methods

EVA - Economic Value Added

The Method of Economic Value Added (EVA) is essentially a system designed to take into account the sources of value creation. The initial objective of the EVA method was to measure the performance of an enterprise. Later, however, it evolved into an important indicator of the calculation of intellectual capital.

It is an important method because it leads business owners and managers to measuring the management of corporate assets. It is a method respected by economic analysts but its complexity and accounting approach make it unreliable.

Positive EVA is interpreted as an additional return on invested capital in relation to the market. It is considered to offer as a final indicator the effectiveness of administrative work over a period of time. For intangible assets it is considered that positive EVA shows us an overall increase in the intellectual capital of the business.

Measurement of intangible value

The Calculated Intangible Value method aims to calculate a business's intellectual capital through seven (7) successive stages.

- *We find the average earnings (before tax) of the last three (3) years,*
- *We measure using the assets from the official financial statements in the last three years by calculating their average,*
- *We discover the profitability of the assets by dividing the profits by the assets of the business,*
- *For the same period (three years) we find the corresponding index of the field,*
- *We multiply the average profitability of the field by the average of tangible fixed assets and the result is subtracted from the average earnings of the last three years,*

- *We calculate the product of the average tax of three years on the additional return deducted from the additional return. That's how we discover the performance of Intellectual Capital,*
- *This return on Intellectual Capital (property) is discounted to the present day, using an appropriate coefficient.*

The final result of the 'intangible value measurement' method if it is magnified from year to year, it shows us that the estimated business is moving better than the competition. The opposite is the case if the index is on a downward path.

15.3.3 Quality indicator methods

Technology Broker

The theoretical basis of the method is based on the logic that the value of a business as a whole constitutes the sum of the intellectual capital (IC) and its tangible (material) assets.

The company is invited to answer twenty (20) questions concerning its intangible assets. The more positive responses are given, the stronger the IC within this. After the twenty (20) questions, more control questions follow, but now for each different intangible asset that the company has.

This approach has opened up new horizons in the process of assessing Intellectual Capital and has received heartfelt criticism from the global community.

Indicative Questions Technology Broker IC Index

- *Do employees know the ultimate purpose of the business;*
- *Is the return on investment measured?*

- *Is there a mechanism to improve the business after customer suggestions?*

IC Control Questions

- *How are patents used?*
- *How does the company identify opportunities for collaboration?*
- *Does the company provide training advice to employees?*

In conclusion, the method presents an overview of the intellectual capital of the company.

Despite the difficulties in its implementation that occur during the process of answering questions, the 'Technology Broker' method has opened up new horizons for exploring the elements of Intellectual Capital.

Balanced Scorecard

The 'balanced scorecard' method was not specifically designed to estimate the value of intangible assets. However, it can be used to measure the intellectual capital of the business and constantly gains the interest of analysts.

It belongs to the category of 'Quality Indicators' and is an important guide for an organized system of reporting, administration and monitoring of corporate results. It was not the first quality indicator proposed for the valuation of Intellectual Capital, but the novelty it brought about was that it introduced a process with a coherent system.

The basis of its theoretical approach is that there are four (4) pillars in each enterprise and it proposes economic and non-economic ways of monitoring them.

- *Customer monitoring that measures performance such as consumer satisfaction etc.*
- *Economic monitoring measuring the progress of economic objectives.*
- *Monitoring learning and development that measures employee data as well as the course of their knowledge.*
- *Monitoring and evaluation of internal processes that measures the possibilities of creating added value.*

All of the above is monitored through quality indicators.

The 'balanced scorecard' method helps businesses, monitor a variety of quality developments. It has been observed that economic data follow the evolution of these qualitative stables!

This method helps to develop the company's strategy and to accept its common vision.

Skandia Navigator Pilot

Skandia's 'Navigator' method is perhaps the most well-known method of measuring intangible assets. Also, this method tries to compare a number of corporate functions and business sectors by monitoring quality indicators.

It considers that corporate value is shaped not simply by numbers, but by a range of factors in five (5) sectors, namely Finance, Clients, Processes, Renewal & Development and Human Capital.

In this context it has developed a number of qualitative indicators covering all of the above five sectors.

Indicative indexes Skandia Navigator

- *Revenue per employee*
- *Revenue from new customers / Total revenue*
- *Profits from new corporate operations*
- *Days of visits to customers*
- *Contact index for sales divided by sales (%)*
- *Number of new customers*
- *PC per Employee*
- *Technology Dynamics / Central Unit*
- *Time to complete proceedings*
- *Customer Satisfaction Index*
- *Training / Administrative Expenses (%)*
- *Average patent age*
- *Managers with a bachelor's degree (%)*
- *Annual degree of staff renewal (%)*
- *Leadership index (%)*

In fact, the 'Navigator' method of Skandia, uses qualitative and quantitative indicators in order to approach the Intellectual Capital.

It believes that there are hidden treasures in every business within human and structural capital, which ultimately make up the corporate dynamics.

It is an ambitious project aimed at driving businesses into the future. It strives to add a strategic vision and encourage all employees to participate in the effort for corporate development.

Intangible Asset Monitor

The 'Intangible Asset Monitoring System' method is another excellent effort to measure the intellectual capital of businesses.

The basis of the method is that the traditional accounting system has been overcome and that new qualitative methods must come to the fore so that the capital of knowledge can be measured and not only that.

It is considered that there is hidden corporate value within three (3) corporate sectors:

α) The external sector (relationships with customers, suppliers, companies, etc.),
b) The Internal sector (administration, process, R&D, IT applications, etc.) and
c) Skills (training, experience, knowledge, etc..).

According to this method, the presentation of official financial statements is not enough and it is necessary to create a new system for measuring and evolving intangible assets that have an equally important role in the modern economy.

The purpose of the method is for the corporate presentation to be made in full, so that all interested parties (investors, shareholders, employees, analysts, etc.) have a complete and holistic knowledge of the course and perspective of the company.

A coherent framework of indicators is therefore proposed with a view to monitoring intangible assets on a consistent basis.

In fact it goes further, by calling for the presentation of the indicators not to be expressed merely by numbers but also to have explanatory observations.

Intangible Asset Monitor Indicators

- *Years of employee experience*
- *Investments in the internal structure*
- *Profitability per customer*
- *Level of education*
- *Investing in information systems*
- *Organic magnification*
- *Customer Satisfaction Index*
- *Proportion of staff with external partners*
- *Sales per employee*
- *Measuring values and behaviours*
- *Proportion of large customers*
- *Profit/loss leverage ratio*
- *Customer value added*
- *Value added per partner*
- *Degree of employee renewal*
- *Degree of youth of workers*
- *Degree of employee loyalty*

- *Personnel age range*
- *Frequency of recurring orders, etc.*

Which indicators will be selected to be monitored and presented, is a decision of each business individually. However, it is necessary to represent all intangible assets and to explain their course.

The 'Intangible Asset Monitoring System' method, offers an in-depth corporate picture. It is another important effort to measure intellectual capital (property) and should not go unnoticed.

15.4 COMMENTS ON METHODS

It is now considered that qualitative models of measurement of intangible assets have taken precedence over financial. This is because they are also seen as tools, to monitor the progress of business administrations and not just to measure intellectual capital.

On the positive side of quality methods, it is measured that the financial community seems to embrace them and adapt them to the requirements of each time, in particular in cases of mergers or acquisitions.

They can also be applied to a number of businesses, regardless of size and market. They can be used even in public sector businesses. However, they still need time to infiltrate in depth and their practical use is not extended.

In fact, there are often no explanatory terms or interpretations, so that neither the indexes nor the value factors affecting intangible assets are understood.

Also due to the nature of the quality factors and due to the fact that they adapt to the specificities of each business, it is not possible to compare with competing businesses of the same field.

A combination of both financial and qualitative valuation models of intangible assets, is necessary in every modern business.

Let's not forget that the final result of each method is often not the complete truth, but is just a specific moment. It is therefore good to monitor both the development (if it increases or decreases), as well as those factors that ultimately are the decisive ones that shape it.

16. GLOBAL INTELLECTUAL PROPERTY ORGANIZATION

But apart from local and regional bodies for the protection of intellectual capital, is there a larger organization? How are such actions and efforts coordinated at global level?

Responses to the above are to be given internationally by The 'World Intellectual Property Organization'. This Agency is one of the sixteen (16) special services of the 'United Nations'.

The 'World Intellectual Property Organization' is an international organization dedicated to promoting the protection of creative innovation of the human spirit. This creation, i.e. intellectual property, broadens the boundaries of science, development and technology and enriches the world of ideas and the arts.

Through its activity, the 'World Intellectual Property Organization' plays an important role in improving the quality and enjoyment of life, as well as in the real wealth of people.

The aim of the organization is to support innovation and the people who promote it and make it a reality. It provides citizens around the world with the right tools to make the most efficient use of their intellectual property. The World Organization for the Protection of Intellectual Property educates thousands of people annually on how to use all this valuable information.

The agency's strategic objectives are indicative of the following:

- *Harmonization of international standards and frameworks for intangible assets and progressive development of international legislation.*

- *Proper communication between the World Intellectual Property Organization and its members in the various states.*
- *Simplifying the use of intellectual capital through the protection of human capital.*
- *Improving infrastructure creation processes for the development of intangible assets.*
- *Creation of sources of information on intellectual capital.*
- *International cooperation to build respect for intangible goods.*

The World Intellectual Property Organization acknowledges Intangible Assets (Intellectual Capital) as the most important goods in more and more powerful businesses worldwide, as they are the main components of market dominance and continued profitability in their business field.

It ultimately highlights Intellectual Capital as the determining factor in the success of acquisitions and merges at global, regional and local level.

The Agency, with its system for the protection of intellectual property, helps to create a more stable environment, in which modernity and creativity can flourish and evolve for the benefit of humanity.

Every day creative people around the world discover new forms of development and improvement of technology, communication and lifestyle in general. The 'World Organization for the Protection of Intellectual Property' is here to assist in this effort, for the benefit of the majority of these people.

17. METHOD OF EXPLOITING THE INTANGIBLE ASSETS BY A BUSINESS

It is necessary for each organization to recognize, investigate and organize its intangible assets (IA), so that it can highlight them and maximize their value.

This effort will bring multiple benefits. Following the workflow below, businesses will become more attractive. All quality factors will work to its advantage and give it comparative advantages leading ultimately to an increase in value!

It is now considered that the value of intangible assets greatly exceeds that of Tangible Assets!

The next challenge for all parties involved is the recognition and establishment of a way of managing, measurement and imaging of these, in the ever-growing Intangible - economic environment!

In particular, the process of management of intangible assets (IA) by businesses should include the following phases:

1. *Recognition & Identification of IA*:

The business is initially called upon to identify and subsequently define – record the intangible assets available to it.

2. *Mapping the "key" forces*.

The business, maps the intangible factors that are consistent with its strategy, studies them and at the same time assesses whether they contribute to the effective implementation of the development path planned by the business.

3. *Measurement of IA:*

The company chooses from a range of models, through which it will value the IA, which it has the ability to use directly or in the long term.

4. *Management of the IA*:

The company shall review, examine, take corrective actions to improve the IA and develop new strategies if necessary.

5. *Providing information*:

The agency ensures the creation of specialized reports on IA in order to monitor them, thus achieving a set of benefits.

Businesses are called to take advantage of the emerging prospects. It is a strategic choice to use intellectual capital, which ultimately becomes an absolute necessity for development and growth.

18. EPILOGUE

The creation of corporate value and the growth of competitive advantages are the main benefits of the exploitation of intangible assets, i.e., the hidden treasures of businesses'. For the reasons we have presented in the book, it is clear that every business with a view to a steady upward trend, must strengthen its intangible assets and in particular the knowledge capital and human resources.

However, this finding does not reflect the reality in modern partnerships. The role of intangible assets in today's knowledge-based economy not only does not have its proper place in the hierarchy of organizations' priorities (regardless of size), but conversely for the leadership of many businesses the content of intellectual capital is 'muddy water'.

An important reason for the current situation is the fact that accounting standards, financial reports and balance sheets, fail to give intellectual capital its true value. This therefore appears to be underestimated, mismanagable, or insufficiently exploited.

In every kind of operational function, however, it is the management of Intangible Assets that is the key to success! The time has come when they can express themselves dynamically through financial statements, presentations and specialized reports.

Why? Because these are the hidden treasures! Let's dig them up, let's show them off, let's sort them out, distinguish and further analyze them, let's put value on our business. We have the ability. Now is the time. Let's dare!

Tangible assets versus intangible assets for S&P 500 companies, 1975-2018 ($bn)

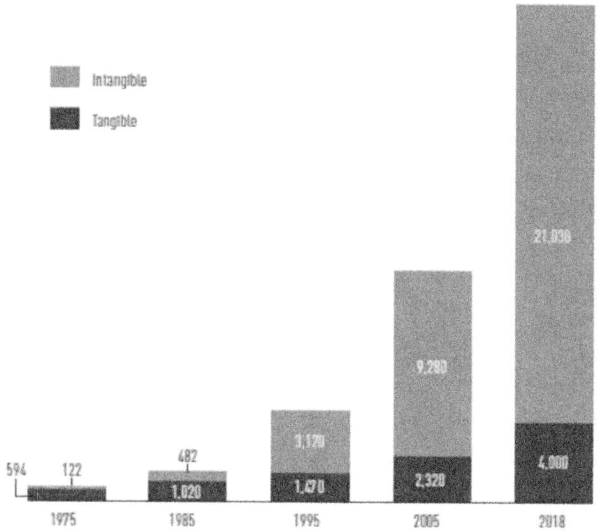

Source: AON. 2019 Intangible Assets Financial Statement Impact Comparison Report. Global edition, April 2019

NOTES

1. *Volkov και Garanina 2007*
2. *Roos 1997*
3. *Bueno 1998*
4. *Jacobsen 2005*
5. *Martínez 2006*
6. *Sveiby 1997*
7. *Sullivan 2000*
8. *American marketing association*
9. *Kallinikos*
10. *Kallinikos*

BIBLIOGRAPHY

- A European Peer Discussion: *Measuring and Managing Intangible Values in Today's Economy,* The New Economy Economics, Finance.
- Aaker D., (1991), *Managing brand equity*, USA: The free press.
- Alafogiannis D., Iliadis O., Spiridonakos I., (2016), *Valuation of business & investment projects*. TEI W. Greece.
- Antonopoulos N., (2019), *Leveraging intangible assets and business development*, University of Pireaus.
- Batsi A., (2001), *Intellectual capital and its valuation by Greek businesses,* Postgraduate thesis, AUTH.
- Bontis, N., Dragonetti, N., Jacobsen, K., Roos, G., (1999), *In The Knowledge Toolbox: A Review of the Tools Available to Measure and Manage Intangible*.
- Bouchoux Deborah, (2018), *Intellectual property*, Cengage learning, USA.
- Cristeas Ch., (2011), *Valuation of enterprises*, Postgraduate thesis, University of Pireaus.
- Damodoran, A., (2012), *Investment Valuation: Tools and Techniques for Determining the Value of Any Asset*, John Wiley & Sons, Inc.
- Dimitriou A., (2007), *Tobin's Q (Q Ratio)*, Postgraduate thesis, University of Pireaus.
- Dr Zimmermann, R., Klein-Bolting, U., Sander, B. and Murad-Aga, T. (2001), *Brand Equity Excellence*, BBDO Group.
- G.I.o.V, (2007), *European evaluation standards*, Athens: Papazisis Publishers.
- Gacathopoulou E., (2014), *Patents and economic growth*, Thesis, University of Pireaus.

- Galbreath, J. (2005), *Which resources matter the most to firm success? An exploratory study of resource-based theory*, Technovation.
- Galbreath, J. and Galvin, P. (2006), *Accounting for performance variation: how important are intangible resources*?, International Journal of Organizational Analysis.
- Godfrey, J. and Koh, P.S. (2001), *The relevance to firm valuation of capitalising intangible assets in total and by category*, Australian Accounting Review.
- Goulias D., (2019), *Creation and development of global brands*, Thesis, University of Macedonia.
- Hegarty R., (2019), *Intellectual property for executives*, USA.
- Hubbard D., (2014), *How to measure anything*, USA: Wiley J. & sons.
- Jennifer M Mueller (2004), *Amortization of Certain Intangible Assets, Journal of Accountancy*, ABI/INFORM Global.
- Kalaintzi P., (2004), *The valuation of the brand*, Postgraduate thesis, University of Macedonia.
- Kaplan R.S., Norton D.P., (1996), *The balanced scorecard: translating strategy into action*, Harvard Business School Press.
- Karagianni I. (2019), *Copyright and internet*, Thesis, DUTH.
- Karakostas I., (2009), *The valuation and registration of intangible assets in the C.A.A.*, Thesis, University of Macedonia.
- Kaufmann L., Schneider Y., (2004), *Intangibles: A synthesis of current research*, Journal of Intellectual Capital.
- Kelvin King, (2017) *The Value of Intellectual Property*, Intangible Assets and Goodwill.
- Kosmopoulos L., (2007), *Valuation of small businesses*, Thesis, University of Pireaus.
- Likostrati M., (2006), *Intangible assets and their contribution to the value of modern business*, University of Macedonia.

- Lindemman, J., Paulter, A. & Smith, A. (2003) *Brands and Branding*. Prices. Journal of Finance.
- Manolopoulou M., (2014), *Accounting and management of intellectual capital*, Ph.D. thesis, University of Patras.
- McWilliam, G. and de Chematony, L., (1991), *'Accounting and Auditing for Brands: What exactly are we valuing?*, Managerial Auditing Journal.
- Mellen C., Evans F., (2018), *Valuation for M&A,* USA: Wiley.
- Mercer C., Harms T., (2020), *Business Valuation, an integrated theory*, USA: Wiley.
- Mercer, Z. C., Crow, M. R. and Patton, K. W., (2002), *'Goodwill Valuation Under SFAS'*, CPA Journal.
- Mikhail Davydov Anna Devyatova, Alexander Shalamov, Ksenia Shneyveys (2016), *Strategy and Management Accounting for Intangible Assets.*
- Moberly Michael, (2014), *safeguarding intangible assets*, Elsevier.
- Nahapiet, J. and Ghoshal, S. (1998), *Social capital, intellectual capital, and the organizational advantage*, Academy of management review.
- Narula, R., and Santangelo, G.D. (2012), *Location and collocation advantages in international innovation*, Multinational Business Review.
- Nelling M., (2011), *Business valuation deMystified*, USA: Mc Graw Hill.
- Pantazis B., (2017), *Valuation of financial companies*, Postgraduate thesis, University of Pireaus.
- Patton, J.R. (2007), *Metrics for knowledge-based project organizations*, Academy of Management Journal.
- Petty Richard, Guthrie James, (2000), *Intellectual capital literature review Measurement, reporting and management*, Journal of Intellectual Capital.
- Prodromidou A., (2013), *International accounting standard 38*, Postgraduate thesis, University of Macedonia.

- Reilly R., (1999), *Valuing intangible assets,* USA: Irwin library.
- Rittas D., (2015), *Human capital as an antidote to the economic crisis,* Postgraduate thesis, University of Macedonia.
- Roos Goran and Roos Johan, (1997), *Measuring your Company's Intellectual Performance*, Long Range Planning.
- Rosenberg N. (1998): *Uncertainty and Technological Change*, United States: Butterworth – Heinemann.
- Saitaki N., (2013), *Intellectual property for small businesses,* IMEGSEVEE.
- Sherman A., (2011), *Harvesting intangible assets,* USA: Amacom.
- Spremann Klaus, (2002), *Finanzanalyse und Unternehmen sbewertung*, Munchen.
- Strassman, P.A. (1999), *The value of knowledge capital.*
- Stweart A. Thomas, (1997), *Intellectual Capital, The new wealth of organisations*, Nicholas Brealey Publishing.
- Tzartzos D., (2018), *Brand Valuation*, Postgraduate thesis, University of Pireaus.
- Tsatsaronis D., (2019), *Trademarks and patents,* Thesis, university of Aegean.
- Webster E. (1999), *The Economics of Intangible Investment,* United Kingdom: Edward Elgar Publishing Limited.

Bibliographic websites

accaglobal.com

accountingtools.com

appraisaleconomics.com

bdc.ca

bloomberg.com

brandfinance.com

brex.com

ecb.europa.eu

ifac.org

investopedia.com

ipe.com

nibusinessinfo.co.uk

oceantomo.com

sciencedirect.com

wipo.int

THE END

Printed in Great Britain
by Amazon

66991033R00088